D0330440

KARATE-DŌ
MY WAY OF LIFE

GICHIN FUNAKOSHI

KODANSHA INTERNATIONAL
Tokyo • New York • London

Distributed in the United States by Kodansha America, Inc.,
114 Fifth Avenue, New York, N.Y. 10011, and in the United
Kingdom and continental Europe by Kodansha Europe
Ltd., 95 Aldwych, London WC2B 4JF.

Published by Kodansha International Ltd., 17-14, Otowa
1-chome, Bunkyo-ku, Tokyo 112, and Kodansha America,
Inc. Copyright © 1975 by Kodansha International Ltd. All
rights reserved. Printed in Japan.

LCC 80-84590
ISBN 0-87011-463-8
ISBN 4-7700-0947-X (in Japan)

First edition, 1975
First paperback edition, 1981
95 96 15 14

CONTENTS

FOREWORD

Much has been published in Japanese about the great karate master, Gichin Funakoshi, but this is the first translation in English of his autobiography. Written not long before his death at the age of ninety, he describes in succinct detail his own life—his childhood and young manhood in Okinawa, his struggle to refine and popularize the art of karate, his prescription for longevity—and reveals his unique personality and his somewhat old-fashioned way of viewing himself, his world and his art.

Through this volume the follower of Karate-dō will gain greater insight into the master's own way of living and thinking and, as a consequence, a sharper understanding of the art of self-defense that he brought to a state of such high perfection. I most heartily recommend these memoirs of Funakoshi not only to those who already practice Karate-dō, or plan to do so, but also to anyone interested in the culture and thought of the Orient.

The origin of karate remains impenetrably hidden behind the mists of legend, but this much we know: it has taken root and is widely practiced throughout East Asia, among peoples who adhere to such varied creeds as Buddhism, Mohammedanism, Hinduism, Brahminism and Taoism. During the course of human history, particular arts of self-defense have gained their own followings in various regions of East Asia, but there is a basic underlying similarity. For this reason karate is related, in one way or another, to the other Oriental arts of self-defense, although (I think it is safe to say) karate is now the most widely practiced of all.

The interrelationship becomes immediately apparent when we compare the impetus behind modern philosophy with that of traditional philosophy. The former has its roots in mathematics, the latter in physical movement and technique. Oriental concepts and ideas, languages and ways of thought have been to a certain extent shaped by their intimate connection with physical skills. Even where words, as well as ideas, have undergone inevitable changes in meaning through the course of human history, we find that their roots remain solidly embedded in physical techniques.

There is a Buddhist saying that, like so many Buddhist sayings, is ostensibly self-contradictory, but for the karate-ka it lends special meaning to his technical practice. Translated, the saying is, "Movement is nonmovement, nonmovement is movement." This is a thesis that, even in contemporary Japan, is accepted by educationalists, and due to its familiarity the saying may even be shortened and used adjectivally in our language.

A Japanese actively seeking self-enlightenment will say that he is "training his stomach" (*hara wo neru*). Although the expression has wide implications, its origin lies in the obvious necessity to harden the muscles of the stomach, a prerequisite for the practice of karate, which is, after all, a combat technique. By bringing the stomach muscles to a state of perfection, a karateka is able to control not only the movements of his hands and feet but also his breathing.

Karate must be nearly as old as man, who early found himself obliged to battle, weaponless, the hostile forces of nature, savage beasts and enemies among his fellow human beings. He soon learned, puny creature that he is, that in his relationship with natural forces accommodation was more sensible than struggle. However, where he was more evenly matched, in the inevitable hostilities with his fellow man, he was obliged to evolve techniques that would enable him to defend himself and, hopefully, to conquer his enemy. To do so, he learned that he had to have a strong and healthy body. Thus, the techniques that he began developing—the techniques that finally became incorporated into Karate-dō—are a ferocious fighting art but are also elements of the all-important art of self-defense.

In Japan, the term *sumō* appears in the nation's most ancient anthology of poetry, the *Man'yōshū*. The sumō of that time (eighth century) included not only the techniques found in present-day sumō but also those of judo and karate, and the latter saw further development under the impetus of Buddhism, since priests used karate as one means of moving toward self-enlightenment. In the seventh and eighth centuries, Japanese Buddhists had journeyed to the Sui and T'ang courts, where they gained insight into the Chinese version of the art and brought back to Japan some of its refinements. For many years, here in Japan, karate remained cloistered behind thick temple walls, in particular those of Zen Buddhism; it was not, apparently, practiced by other people until samurai began to train within temple compounds and so came to learn of the existence of the art. Karate as we know it today has been perfected within the last half century by Gichin Funakoshi.

There are innumerable delightful anecdotes about this

extraordinary man, many of which he recounts himself in the pages that follow. Some have perhaps by now drifted into the realm of legend, and some Funakoshi did not bother to tell because they were so intimate a part of his way of life that he was hardly aware of them. He never deviated from his way of life, the way of the samurai. Perhaps to the young Japanese of the postwar world, almost as much as to the foreign reader, Funakoshi will emerge as something of an eccentric, but he was merely following the moral and ethical code of his ancestors, a code that existed long before there was such a thing as written history in Okinawa.

He observed the age-old taboos. For example, to a man of his class the kitchen was forbidden territory, and Funakoshi, so far as I know, never trespassed upon it. Nor did he ever bother to utter the names of such mundane articles as socks or toilet paper, for—once again in the code that he rigorously followed—these were associated with what was considered to be improper or indecent.

To those of us who studied under him he was a great and revered master, but I fear that in the eyes of his young grandson Ichirō (now a colonel in the Air Self-Defense Force) he was merely a very stubborn old man. I well recall an occasion when Funakoshi spied a pair of socks lying on the floor. With a gesture toward Ichirō, he said, "Put those away!"

"But I don't undersand," said Ichirō with a look of utter innocence. "What do you mean by 'those'?"

"Yes," said Funakoshi, "those, *those!*"

"Those, *those!*" Ichirō retorted. "Don't you know the word for 'those'?"

"I said to put those away immediately!" Funakoshi

repeated, and Ichirō was forced to admit defeat. His little trap had failed; his grandfather still adamantly refused, as he had all his life, to utter the word for socks.

In the course of his book Funakoshi describes some of his daily habits. For example, the first thing he did upon arising in the morning was to brush and comb his hair, a process that sometimes occupied an entire hour. He used to say that a samurai must always be neat in appearance. After having made himself presentable, he would turn toward the Imperial Palace and bow deeply; then he would turn in the direction of Okinawa and perform a similar bow. Only after these rites were completed would he sip his morning tea.

Well, my purpose here is not to tell his story for him, merely to introduce him. And that I am very happy and proud to do. Master Funakoshi was a splendid example of a man of his rank born at the beginning of the Meiji period, and there are few men left in Japan today who may be said to observe a similar code. I am very grateful to have been one of his disciples and can only regret that he is no longer with us.

GENSHIN HIRONISHI, PRESIDENT
JAPAN KARATE-DŌ SHŌTŌ-KAI

PREFACE

It was nearly four decades ago that I embarked upon what I now realize was a highly ambitious program: the introduction to the Japanese public at large of that complex Okinawan art, or sport, which is called Karate-dō, "the Way of Karate." These forty years have been turbulent ones, and the path that I chose for myself turned out to be far from easy; now, looking back, I am astonished that I attained in this endeavor even the quite modest success that has come my way.

That Karate-dō has now taken its place in the world as an internationally recognized sport is due wholly to the efforts of my masters, my fellow practitioners, my friends and my students, all of whom have unstintingly devoted both time and effort to the task of refining this art of self-defense to its present state of perfection. As for my own role, I feel it has been no more that of an introducer—a master of ceremonies, so to speak, one who was blessed by both time and chance to appear at the opportune moment.

It is no exaggeration to say that almost all the ninety years of my life have been devoted to Karate-dō. I was rather a sickly baby and a frail child; accordingly, it was suggested when I was still quite young that to overcome these handicaps I ought to begin the study of karate. This I did, but with little interest at the very first. However, during the latter half of my years at primary school, after my health began to improve noticeably, my interest in karate began to grow. Soon, I found, it had cast a spell over me. Into the task of mastering it I threw myself mind and body, heart and soul. I had been a frail, irresolute, introverted child; by the time I reached manhood, I felt myself to be strong, vigorous and outgoing.

As I look back over the nine decades of my life—from childhood to youth to maturity to (making use of an expression that I dislike) old age—I realize that it is thanks to my devotion to Karate-dō that I have never once had to consult a physician. I have never in my life taken any medicine: no pills, no elixirs, not even a single injection. In recent years my friends have accused me of being immortal; it is a joke to which I can only reply, seriously but simply, that my body had been so well trained that it repels all sickness and disease.

In my opinion, there are three kinds of ailments that afflict a human being: illnesses that cause fever, malfunctions of the gastrointestinal system and physical injuries. Almost invariably, the cause of a disability is rooted in an unwholesome life-style, in irregular habits, and in poor circulation. If a man who runs a temperature practices karate until the sweat begins to pour from his body, he will soon find that his temperature has dropped to normal, and that his illness has been cured. If a man with gastric troubles does the same, it will cause his blood to circulate more freely and so alleviate his distress. Physical injuries are, of course, another matter, but many of these too may be avoided by a well-trained man exercising proper care and caution. Karate-dō is not merely a sport that teaches how to strike and kick; it is also a defense against illness and disease.

Only recently has it attained international popularity, but this is a popularity that karate teachers must foster and use with great care. It has been very gratifying to me to see the enthusiasm with which young men and women, and even children, have taken to the sport, not only in my own country but all over the world.

That, no doubt, is one of the reasons that the *Sangyō Keizai Shimbun* ("Journal of Commerce and Industry") has asked me to write about Karate-dō. Initially I replied that I am an old man and a plain ordinary citizen, with very little to say. However, it is true that I have dedicated virtually my entire life to Karate-dō, so I have accepted the newspaper's offer on the condition that the editors permit me to write a sort of autobiography.

At the same time, setting about the task, I feel rather embarrassed, so I must ask my readers to forgive me for speaking of such inconsequential matters. I ask them to regard my book as little more than the ravings of a very old man. I, for my part, will stir these ancient bones of mine and, with the help of my readers, focus my energies on uncovering the great law of heaven and earth for the sake of the nation and of future generations. In pursuing this endeavor I beg the wholehearted support and co-operation of my readers.

I would like to express here my gratitude to Hiroshi Irikata of the *Weekly Sankei Magazine*, for his editorial assistance, and to Toyohiko Nishimura of the same magazine, for his book design [of the Japanese edition].

GICHIN FUNAKOSHI

Tokyo
September, 1956

ENTERING THE WAY

Losing a Topknot

The Meiji Restoration and I were born in the same year, 1868. The former saw the light of day in the shogun's former capital of Edo, which came to be known as Tokyo. I was born in the district of Yamakawa-chō in the royal Okinawan capital of Shuri. If anyone were to take the trouble to consult official records, he would learn that I was born in the third year of Meiji (1870), but the true facts are that my birth occurred in the first year of the reign and that I had to falsify my official record so as to be allowed to sit for entrance examinations to a Tokyo medical school.

At that time, there was a regulation that only those born in the year 1870 or thereafter could be considered qualified to take the examinations, so I had no alternative but to tamper with the official records, which was easier to do then because, strange as it may seem, registration was not so strict as it is today.

Having thus altered the date of my birth, I sat for the examinations and passed them, but still I did not enter the Tokyo medical school. The cause, which seemed very reasonable then, would seem rather less so now, I imagine.

Among the many reforms instituted by the young Meiji government during the first twenty years of its life was the abolition of the topknot, a masculine hairstyle that had been a traditional part of Japanese life for much longer than anyone could possibly remember. In Okinawa, in particular, the topknot was considered a symbol not simply of maturity and virility but of manhood itself. As the edict banning the revered topknot was nationwide, there was opposition to it throughout the country, but nowhere, I think, were the lines of battle so fiercely drawn as in Okinawa.

Here those who believed that the future destiny of Japan required it to adopt Western ideas and those who believed the opposite were at constant loggerheads on almost every reform instituted by the government. Nothing, however, seemed to stir Okinawans to such heights of frenzy as the question of the abolition of the topknot. In general, men born into the *shizoku* (or privileged) class were obstinately opposed, while those of the *heimin* (or common) class as well as a few of the *shizoku* supported what might be called the abolition bill. The latter group was known as the *Kaika-tō* (the "Enlightenment Party"), the former the *Ganko-tō* (literally, the "Obstinate Party").

My family had for generations been attached to a lower-ranking official, and the whole clan was unanimously and adamantly opposed to the cutting of the topknot. Such an act was utterly abhorrent to every member of my family, although I myself did not feel strongly one way or the other. The outcome was that I bowed to family pressure, for the school refused to accept students who persisted in the traditional style, and thus the whole future course of my life was influenced by so slight a matter as a bushy topknot.

Eventually, of course, like everyone else, I was to conform, but before I tell how that came about, I must go back a few years in time. My father Gisu was a minor

2   ENTERING THE WAY

official, and I was his only son. Born prematurely, I was rather a sickly baby, and since both parents and grand-parents agreed that I was not destined to a long life, they all took special care of me. In particular, I was coddled and pampered by both pairs of grandparents. Indeed, not long after my birth I was taken to live with my mother's parents, and there my grandfather taught me the Four Chinese Classics and Five Chinese Classics of the Con-fucian tradition—essential for the sons of the *shizoku*.

It was during my stay at my grandparents' home that I began attending primary school, and after a time I became close friends with one of my classmates. This too was des-tined to alter the course of my life (and in a far more fundamental way than the topknot), for my classmate was the son of Yasutsune Azato, a most amazing man who was one of Okinawa's greatest experts in the art of karate.

Master Azato belonged to one of the two upper classes of shizoku families in Okinawa: the Udon were of the highest class and were equivalent to daimyo among clans outside of Okinawa; the Tonochi were hereditary chiefs of towns and villages. It was to the latter group that Azato belonged, his family occupying this exalted position in the village of Azato, located between Shuri and Naha. So great was their prestige that the Azatos were treated not as vassals by the former governor of Okinawa but rather as close friends on an equal footing.

Master Azato not only was unsurpassed in all Okinawa in the art of karate but also excelled in horsemanship, in Japanese fencing (*kendō*), and in archery. He was, more-over, a brilliant scholar. It was my good fortune to be brought to his attention and eventually to receive my first instruction in karate at his remarkable hands.

At that time the practice of karate was banned by the government, so sessions had to take place in secret, and pupils were strictly forbidden by their teachers to discuss with anyone the fact that they were learning the art. I shall have more to say on this subject later on; for the moment, suffice it to note that karate practice could then be held only at night and only in secret. Azato's house was situated quite a distance from that of my grandparents, where I was still living, but once my enthusiasm for the art began to take hold I never found that nighttime walk too long. It was after a couple of years' practice that I realized my health had improved tremendously, and that I was no longer the frail child I had been. I enjoyed karate but—more than that—I felt deeply indebted to the art for my increased well-being, and it was around this time that I began to seriously consider making Karate-dō a way of life.

However, the thought did not enter my mind that it might also become a profession, and since the thorny topknot controversy had put a medical career beyond my reach, I now began to consider alternatives. As I had been taught the Chinese classics from early childhood by both my grandfather and Azato, I decided to make use of that knowledge by becoming a schoolteacher. Accordingly, I took the qualifying examinations and was granted a position as assistant instructor at a primary school. My first experience in taking charge of a classroom occurred in 1888, when I was twenty-one years old.

But the topknot still obtruded, for before I could be permitted to enter upon my duties as a teacher I was required to get rid of it. This seemed to me entirely reasonable. Japan was then in a state of great ferment; tremen-

4   ENTERING THE WAY

dous changes were occurring everywhere, along every facet of life. I felt that I, as a teacher, had an obligation to help our younger generation, which would one day forge the destiny of our nation, to bridge the wide gaps that yawned between the old Japan and the new. I could hardly object to the official edict that our traditional topknot had now become a relic of the past. Nevertheless, I trembled when I thought about what the older members of my family would say.

At that time, schoolteachers wore official uniforms (not unlike those worn by students in the Peers' School before the last war), a dark jacket buttoned up to the neck, the brass buttons embossed with a cherry blossom design, and a cap with a badge that also bore a cherry blossom design. It was while wearing this uniform, having been shorn of my topknot, that I paid a visit to my parents to report that I had been employed as an assistant instructor in a primary school.

My father could hardly believe his eyes. "What have you done to yourself?" he cried angrily. "You, the son of a samurai!" My mother, even angrier than he, refused to speak to me. She turned away, left the house through the back door, and fled to her parents' home. I imagine all this hullabaloo must strike the youth of today as almost inconceivably ridiculous.

In any case, the die had been cast. Despite all the strenuous parental objection, I entered the profession that I was to follow for the next thirty years. But I by no means abandoned my first true love. I taught school during the day and then, as the ban against karate was still being enforced, I made my stealthy way in the dead of night, carrying a dim lantern when there was no moon, to the house of Master Azato. When, night after night, I would steal home just before daybreak, the neighbors took to conjecturing among themselves as to where I went and what I was doing. Some decided that the only possible answer to this curious enigma was a brothel.

The truth of the matter was very different indeed. Night after night, often in the backyard of the Azato house as the master looked on, I would practice a *kata* ("formal exercise") time and again week after week, sometimes month after month, until I had mastered it to my teacher's satisfaction. This constant repetition of a single kata was grueling, often exasperating and on occasion humiliating. More than once I had to lick the dust on the floor of the dōjō or in the Azato backyard. But practice was strict, and I was never permitted to move on to another kata until Azato was convinced that I had satisfactorily understood the one I had been working on.

Although considerably advanced in years, he always sat ramrod stiff on the balcony when we worked outside, wearing a *hakama*, with a dim lamp beside him. Quite often, through sheer exhaustion, I found myself unable to make out even the lamp.

After executing a kata, I would await his verbal judgment. It was always terse. If he remained dissatisfied with my technique, he would murmur, "Do it again," or, "A little more!" A little more, a little more, so often a little more, until the sweat poured and I was ready to drop: it was his way of telling me there was still something to be learned, to be mastered. Then, if he found my progress satisfactory, his verdict would be expressed in a single word, "Good!" That one word was his highest praise. Until I had heard it spoken several times, however, I

6   ENTERING THE WAY

would never dare ask him to begin teaching a new kata.

But after our practice sessions ended, usually in the small hours of the morning, he would become a different kind of teacher. Then he would theorize about the essence of karate or, like a kindly parent, question me about my life as a schoolteacher. As the night was drawing to a close, I would take my lantern and head for home, conscious as my journey ended of the suspicious eyes of the neighbors.

I must under no circumstances omit mention of a good friend of Azato, a man who was also born to a shizoku family of Okinawa and who was considered to be as proficient in karate as Azato himself. Sometimes I would practice under the tutelage of the two masters, Azato and Itosu, at the same time. On these occasions I would listen most attentively to the discussions between the two, and by doing so I learned a great deal about the art in its spiritual as well as its physical aspects.

Were it not for these two great masters I would be a very different person today. I find it almost impossible to express my gratitude to them for guiding me along the path that has provided my chief source of gratification during eight decades of life.

Recognizing Nonsense

I feel that it is essential, right here at the start, to insert a brief comment about what karate is *not*, for there has been so much nonsense written on the subject in recent years. Later on, as the occasion arises, I shall attempt to make clear what karate in fact *is*. But before going any further I think it only right to sweep away some of the misconceptions that continue to obscure the essential nature of the art.

Once, for example, I heard someone who professed to be an authority tell his astonished listeners that "in karate we have a kata called *nukite*. Using only the five fingers of one hand, a man may penetrate his adversary's rib cage, take hold of the bones, and tear them out of the body. This is, of course," the so-called authority went on, "a very difficult kata to master. One begins to train for it by thrusting one's fingers into a cask full of beans every day for hours and hours, thousands upon thousands of times. At first one's fingers will become lacerated by the exercise, and one's hand will bleed. Then, as time after time the blood coagulates, the shape of one's fingers will alter grotesquely.

"Eventually the sensation of pain will disappear. Then the beans in the cask must be replaced by sand, for sand of course is more unyielding and the fingers encounter much greater resistance. Nonetheless, as the training proceeds, the fingers will eventually pierce the sand and reach the bottom of the cask. After training with sand comes training with pebbles, until here too after long practice success is attained. Finally comes training with pellets of lead. At last, with lengthy and strenuous training sessions, the fingers will have become strong enough not only to shatter a thick slab of wood but also to crush with little difficulty a heavy stone or pierce the hide of a horse."

No doubt many who heard this strange exposition came away believing it. Many students of karate still choose, for one reason or another, to foster such myths. For example, a man who is relatively unfamiliar with the art may say to an adept: "I understand that you practice karate. Tell me, can you really shatter a huge rock with your fingers? Can you really make a hole in a man's belly with them?" Should the adept reply that either one of those two feats is quite impossible, he would be telling no more than the naked truth. Yet there are some adepts, or pretended adepts, who will shrug deprecatingly and murmur, "Well, sometimes I . . ." As a result, the layman receives a totally false, and indeed intimidating, impression of the art; he wonders, with both fear and awe, if the adept has acquired superhuman powers.

The fact is that the karate enthusiast who overstates and exaggerates and indeed perverts the nature of the art is a skillful conversationalist, true enough, and he will certainly succeed in fascinating his listeners and convincing them that karate is something frightful. But what he is saying is utterly untrue, and furthermore he knows it. As to why he does it—well, it sounds good.

Perhaps, in the distant past, there were karate experts capable of performing such miraculous feats. To that I cannot testify, but I can assure my readers that, at least to my fairly wide knowledge, there is no man living who, however much he may have trained and practiced, can exceed the natural bounds of human powers.

Yet there are adepts who continue to claim otherwise. "In karate," they say, "a strong grip is essential. To acquire it one must practice hour after hour. The best way is, using the tips of the fingers of both hands, to pick up two heavy buckets, preferably full of something like sand, and swing them around many, many times. The man who has strengthened his grip to the maximum in this way is easily capable of ripping the flesh of his adversary into strips."

What nonsense! One day such a man came to my dōjō and offered to teach me the secret of ripping flesh into strips. I begged him to demonstrate on me but burst into laughter when, at last, he succeeded in pinching my skin a bit without even causing a single black-and-blue mark.

Now, it goes without saying that a strong grip is of great advantage to the practitioner of karate. I recall hearing of a man who could circle his house in Okinawa by swinging along the eaves—no mean feat, as anyone will realize who knows Okinawan houses. I myself have seen Master Itosu crush a thick bamboo stem in his bare hand. This may seem a prodigious feat, but it is my belief that his remarkably strong grip was a natural gift, not acquired by training alone, although obviously enhanced by it. Any man will be able, after sufficient practice, to accomplish remarkable feats of strength, but he may go only so far and no farther. There is a limit to human physical strength that no one can exceed.

While it is true that a karate expert has the power to break a thick board or several layers of tile with one stroke of his hand, I assure my readers that anyone is capable of doing the same thing after undergoing sufficient training. There is nothing extraordinary about such an accomplishment.

Nor has it anything whatsoever to do with the true spirit of karate; it is merely a demonstration of the kind of strength that a man may acquire through practice. There is nothing mysterious about it. I am often asked by people unfamiliar with karate whether the ranking of an adept depends upon the number of boards or tiles he is capable of breaking with one slash of his hand. There is, of course, no relation whatsoever between the two. Inasmuch as karate is one of the most refined of the martial arts, any karate adept who boasts about how many boards or tiles he can break with his bare hand or who claims to be able to rip flesh into strips or tear ribs from their cage is one who has very little conception of what true karate is.

The Teacher

At the time I began my academic career, there were four categories of primary school instructors: those who taught the most elementary classes, those who instructed higher grades, those who had charge of special courses and those who served as assistants. At that time, four years of primary school education were compulsory. Teachers in the first category had classes in the first and second grades, while teachers in the more advanced category were qualified to take the last two compulsory grades, the third and fourth, as well as the upper grades (five through eight), which were not compulsory.

Although I was first hired as an assistant, not long thereafter I passed the examinations that qualified me to act as a lower-grade instructor. I was then transferred to Naha, the seat of the Okinawan prefectural government. This transfer, which was in fact a promotion, I considered to be a most fortunate thing, as it allowed me more time and greater opportunity for karate practice.

Later, I also qualified as an instructor in the higher grades. Since, however, I was not a graduate of a teacher's training college and an increasing number of such graduates were entering the Okinawan school system, I realized that further promotion was going to be a very slow process.

At length, the principal of my school recommended that I be advanced to a higher post. This particular promotion I turned down, for acceptance would have meant going to outlying districts or remote islands in the archipelago and, consequently, separation from my karate teachers. This I could not possibly accept.

There was, in fact, another reason why I was permitted by my superiors to remain in Naha, which brings us once again to the controversy that raged about the topknot. The families of many of my pupils were staunch supporters of the Obstinate Party, and although we were by now in the twenty-fourth or twenty-fifth year of Meiji (1891 or 1892), the government edict banning the topknot was far from being faithfully observed in Okinawa. Inasmuch as my own family also supported the Obstinate Party, I could well understand the emotion that prompted this defiance of the government's orders. At the same time, aware of the tremendous reforms that were changing virtually every aspect of Japanese life, I could not but regard the matter as of little importance.

The Ministry of Education, however, did not see things in the same light. Appalled by Okinawan resistance to its will, it decreed that every pupil on the island must be shorn of his topknot forthwith. This was not quite so easy a matter as it may sound, for many children, insistent upon retaining their topknot, had delayed their entry into primary school as long as possible. The result was that they were hardly children any longer, and they were more than a match for their scissors-wielding teachers. Moreover, many of them had trained in karate, which was then being practiced more openly in Okinawa. Primary school teachers, seeking to impose their will on these

12   ENTERING THE WAY

"children," sometimes found the shears entirely useless.

It was for this reason that instructors who were familiar with karate were given the task of coping with obstinate topknotted pupils who were also karate adepts. I can still recall the sight of pupils, captured after a lively scuffle, submitting to the odious shears with tears in their eyes and their fists tightly clenched as though they would like nothing better than to annihilate the despoilers of those tokens of manhood. However, it was not long before all our boys had their heads closely shaved. The topknot furor had ended forever.

Meanwhile, I continued assiduously with my karate, training under a number of teachers: Master Kiyuna, who with his bare hands could strip the bark from a living tree in a matter of moments; Master Tōonno of Naha, one of the island's best-known Confucian scholars; Master Niigaki, whose great common sense impressed me most deeply; and Master Matsumura, one of the greatest ka-rateka, about whom I will have more to say later. This is not to say that I neglected either of my first two masters. On the contrary, I spent as much time with them as possible, and from them I learned not only karate but a great deal else besides.

Master Azato, for example, was an extremely astute observer of political affairs. I recall his saying to me once, "Funakoshi, after the Trans-Siberian Railroad is completed, war between Japan and Russia will become inevitable." This was many years before the outbreak of hostilities between the two countries in 1904. What had once seemed unlikely became actuality, and I found myself, once war broke out, deeply impressed by Azato's political acumen and foresight. It was he who, at the time of the Meiji Restoration, advised the governor of Okinawa to cooperate to the fullest with the newly formed government, and when the edict against the topknot was promulgated, he was among the first to obey it.

Azato was also a highly skilled fencer of the Jigen school of *kendō*. Although by no means a braggart, he had utter confidence in his fencing ability, and I once heard him say, "I doubt very much that I would lose to anyone in the country if it came to a duel to the death." This quiet confidence was later proved to be well founded when Azato met Yōrin Kanna, one of Okinawa's most famous swordsmen.

Kanna was an enormous, muscular man with great bulging arms and shoulders; indeed, people used to say that his shoulder muscles were two stories high! He was a brave man and utterly without fear, and he well merited his reputation for proficiency in the martial arts. He was also a man of great learning, thoroughly at home in both the Japanese and Chinese classics. Clearly, one would have thought, he was more than a match for Azato.

However when, in the famous encounter, he attacked Azato with an unblunted blade, he was very much surprised to find his attack turned aside by his unarmed adversary, who, with a deft flip of his hand, not only managed to evade the thrust but also brought Kanna to his knees. When I asked Azato to describe for me what had actually occurred, he described Kanna as a highly skilled swordsman who, due to his reputation of being both indomitable and fearless, was able to terrify his opponent at the very start of the encounter and then come in quickly for the kill. However, Azato said, if the opponent refuses to be terrified, if he remains coolheaded, and if he searches for the inevitable gap in Kanna's defense, victory cannot be all that difficult. This counsel, like all the rest of Azato's guidance, was to prove of great value to me.

Another of his maxims was, "When you practice karate, think of your arms and legs as swords." Indeed, Azato's own exhibitions of karate were living examples of this philosophy. Once a man asked him the meaning and application of *ippon-ken* (single-point fist). "Try to hit me," Azato replied calmly. The man did as he had been told, but in the twinkling of an eye the blow was parried and Azato's own single-point fist flew toward his opponent's stomach, where it stopped, at a distance of perhaps the thickness of a sheet of paper. The celerity of the whole movement was incredible. The man who had asked the question did not even have time to blink his eyes before he realized that that fist, had it actually struck his solar plexus, might well have killed him.

Azato had highly detailed information about all karate experts living in Okinawa at the time, which included not only such mundane facts as their names and addresses but also intelligence about their abilities and their special skills and techniques, where they were strong and where they were weak. He used to tell me that knowledge of an opponent's ability and his technical skills was half the battle, quoting the old Chinese adage, "The secret of victory is to know both yourself and your enemy."

Both Azato and his good friend Itosu shared at least one quality of greatness: they suffered from no petty jealousy of other masters. They would present me to the teachers of their acquaintance, urging me to learn from each the technique at which he excelled. Ordinary karate instructors, in my experience, are reluctant to permit their pupils to study under instructors of other schools, but this was far from true of either Azato or Itosu.

If they had taught me nothing else, I would have profited by the example they set of humility and modesty in all dealings with their fellow human beings. And, indeed, they never dwelled upon the "heroic" deeds of karate that were attributed to them, brushing these aside as "wild acts" attributable to their youth.

The two men shared other qualities, including, interestingly enough, a first name, Yasutsune. But philosophically they held quite divergent points of view regarding karate, and physically they were very different indeed. While Master Azato was tall with broad shoulders and had sharp eyes and features reminiscent of the ancient samurai, Master Itosu was of average height, with a great round chest like a beer barrel. Despite his long moustache, he rather had the look of a well-behaved child.

It was a deceptive look, for his arms and hands possessed quite extraordinary power. However many times he was challenged by Azato to a bout of Okinawan hand wrestling, he always emerged victorious. In this particular version of the sport, the two combatants clench their fists and cross their wrists one against the other; they do not clasp hands as they would in a bout of the Tokyo version of hand wrestling. After being inevitably overpowered, Azato would murmur wryly that never would he get the better of Itosu—not even, he would add, if he used both hands.

Indeed, Itosu was so well trained that his entire body seemed to be invulnerable. Once, as he was about to enter a restaurant in Naha's amusement center, a sturdy young

ENTERING THE WAY

man attacked him from the rear, aiming a hearty blow at his side. But the latter, without even turning, hardened the muscles of his stomach so that the blow glanced off his body, and at the very same instant his right hand grasped the right wrist of his assailant. Still without turning his head, he calmly dragged the man inside the restaurant.

There, he ordered the frightened waitresses to bring food and wine. Still holding the man's wrist with his right hand, he took a sip of the wine from the cup that he held in his left hand, then pulled his assailant around in front of him and for the first time had a look at him. After a moment, he smiled and said, "I don't know what your grudge against me could be, but let's have a drink together!" The young man's astonishment at this behavior can easily be imagined.

Itosu had another famous encounter with a rash young man, this one the karate instructor of a certain Okinawan school. Belligerent by nature and full of pride at his strength, the youth had the rather unpleasant habit of lurking in dark lanes, and when a lonely walker happened to come strolling by he would lash out at the poor man. So self-confident did he finally become that he decided to take on Itosu himself, believing that, no matter how powerful the master was, he could be beaten if set upon unawares.

One night, he followed Itosu down the street and, after a stealthy approach, aimed his mightiest punch at the master's back. Bewildered by the quite evident fact that he had made no impression whatsoever, the young bully lost his balance and at that same instant felt his right wrist caught in a viselike grip. The youth tried to free himself with his other hand, but of course he did not succeed. The power of Itosu's grip was proverbial in Okinawa; he could, as I recounted earlier, crush a thick bamboo stalk with one hand.

Itosu now walked on, hauling the other behind him without even bothering to look back. Realizing that he had failed completely, the young man begged the master's forgiveness. "But who are you?" Itosu asked softly.

"I'm Gorō," replied the youth. Now Itosu looked at him for the first time.

"Ah," he murmured, "you really shouldn't try to play such tricks on an old man like me." With that, he let go and strolled away.

Vivid pictures jostle one another in my mind as I think back about my two teachers and their different philosophies of Karate-dō. "Regard your arms and legs as swords," Azato used to tell me, while Itosu would advise me to train my body so that it could withstand any blow, no matter how powerful. What he meant, of course, was that I not only must train my body until it became as hard as nails but also must practice daily all the various karate techniques.

I now recall a well-known incident when Itosu was set upon by a group of young toughs, but before long the hoodlums were all lying unconscious in the street. An eyewitness, seeing that Itosu was in no danger, rushed off to tell Azato about the incident. Interrupting his account, Azato said, "And the ruffians, of course, were all lying unconscious, with their faces to the ground, were they not?" Much surprised, the witness admitted that that was true, but he wondered how Azato could have known.

"Very simple," replied the master. "No karate adept

would be so cowardly as to attack from the rear. And should someone unfamiliar with karate attack from the front, he would end up flat on his back. But I know Itosu; his punches would knock his assailants down on their faces. I would be quite astonished if any of them survive."

Another time, Itosu was awakened during the night by some suspicious noises at the gate of his house. As he moved silently toward the sound, he realized that someone was trying to pick the lock of his gate. Without a moment's pause, he shattered the gate's wooden panel with a single blow of his fist. Simultaneously he thrust his hand through the hole and caught hold of the wrist of the would-be robber. Now normally, if the average karateka had punched a hole through a thick wooden panel, the hole would be jagged and the wood would splinter in one direction or another. In this particular case, there was only a round hole, and I know that to be true because I was told so by Azato himself.

I have always been conscious of the compliment paid me by these two masters. In return I performed a rite—not only in their honor but in honor of all masters who have ever taught me—which I recommend to every student of karate today: I burned incense at the Buddhist altar of each instructor and pledged myself never to make use of my trained body for any illicit purpose. I think it was this pledge, which I have most faithfully honored, that resulted in my being treated like a member of the family, long after I myself was married and had children of my own—indeed, until the deaths of the two older men.

I frequently took my children to their homes, where on these occasions they would demonstrate certain kata for the children and then bid them to do the same. As a treat, the two masters would give my children sweets of a kind that I could not myself afford to buy for them. (The best I could do at that time was an occasional sweet potato!) The masters loved the young ones and behaved toward them as to their own grandchildren. Soon the youngsters began to visit the masters by themselves, just as I had done when I was a child. And soon they came to love karate as I did.

Now that I look back, I realize that I and my children, the two generations of us, have all benefited enormously from the teachings of these two masters. Where shall I find words to express my gratitude?

NO WEAPONS

An Important Lesson

Among the Okinawan teachers under whom I studied from time to time was Master Matsumura, about whom a famous story is told: how he defeated another master in a bout without even striking a blow. So famous is the story, in fact, that it is now legendary; nevertheless, I should like to retell it here, for it is an unparalleled expression of the true meaning of karate.

Let us begin, then, in the fairly humble shop of a Naha man who earned his living engraving designs on objects of daily use. Although he had already passed his fortieth birthday, he was still in the very prime of his manhood: his great neck had the massive quality of a bull's. Beneath the short sleeves of his kimono his muscles bulged and rippled, his cheeks were full, and his face was as bronzed as copper. Clearly, although a modest artisan, he was a man to be reckoned with.

Into his shop one day there came a man of an altogether different stamp but one who was also, just as clearly, a man of great fighting spirit. He was younger than the engraver, in his late twenties one might have guessed, certainly no more than thirty, and his physical presence, although it lacked the massiveness of the engraver's, was nonetheless imposing. He was very tall, six feet at least, but his most striking feature was his eyes: they were as sharp and piercing as the eyes of an eagle. Yet as he made his way into the engraver's little workroom, he was pale and appeared dejected.

His voice was subdued as he told the engraver he wanted a design engraved on the brass bowl of his long-stemmed pipe.

As he took the pipe into his hands, the engraver said in very polite terms, for he was clearly of a lower social class than his visitor, "I beg your pardon, sir, but aren't you Matsumura, the karate teacher?"

"Yes," came the laconic reply. "What of it?"

"Ah, I knew I could not have been mistaken! For a long time now I have been hoping that I might study karate with you."

But the younger man's reply was curt. "Sorry," he said. "I no longer teach."

The engraver, however, persisted. "You teach the head of the clan himself, don't you?" he asked. "Everyone says you are the finest karate instructor in the land."

"I have indeed taught him," the young visitor replied bitterly, "but it's not my habit to teach others. And in point of fact I no longer teach the head of the clan either. To tell you the truth," he burst out, "I'm fed up to the teeth with karate!"

"What an extraordinary thing to say!" cried the engraver. "How can a man of your caliber be fed up with karate? Would you be so kind as to tell me why?"

"I couldn't care less," muttered the young man, "whether I teach karate to the head of the clan or not. Indeed, it was through trying to teach him karate that I lost my job."

"I don't understand," said the engraver. "Everyone knows you're the best instructor alive, and if you're no

22

longer teaching him, who is? Surely no one can take your place."

"Indeed," Matsumura answered, "it was because of my reputation that I was granted the post of instructor to the head of the clan. But he was an indifferent student. He neglected the refinement of his techniques, which, despite all my efforts, remained very crude. Oh, I could have lost to him easily if I chose, but that would hardly have been of any use to him, so instead I pointed out some of his weaknesses and then I dared him to attack me with all his might. He countered instantly with a double kick (*nidan-geri*). It was dextrous enough, I grant you, but I hardly need to tell you that only a rank novice would open with a double kick when facing an opponent he knew to be vastly more competent.

"I decided to make use of this error to teach him a much needed lesson. As you must know, a karate match is a matter of life and death, and once you have made a serious mistake you are done for. It's impossible to recover. You know all this yourself quite well. But apparently he did not, and so, hoping to show him the truth, I at once stopped his double kick with my sword hand and sent him sprawling. But before he actually struck the floor I crashed my body against his. He finally came to rest in a heap at least six yards away."

"Was he badly hurt?" asked the engraver.

"His shoulder. His hand. His leg, where my sword hand struck it, turned all black and blue." The young man was silent for a moment. Then he went on. "For quite a long while, he couldn't even get up from the floor."

"How terrible!" cried the engraver. "Of course you were reprimanded?"

"Of course. I was commanded to leave at once and not to reappear until further notice."

"I see," said the engraver thoughtfully. "But surely he will pardon you."

"I think not. Although the incident took place more than a hundred days ago, I have heard nothing further from him. I am told he is still very angry with me and says that I am far too arrogant. No, I doubt very much that he will grant me a pardon. Ah," murmured the master, "it would have been better for me had I never attempted to teach karate to the head of the clan in the first place. In fact, I'd have been better off had I never learned karate myself!"

"Nonsense!" said the engraver. "In every man's life there are ups and downs. But," he added, "since you're no longer teaching him, why don't you teach me?"

"No!" said Matsumura curtly. "I've given up teaching. In any case, why should a man like you, with a reputation as an expert, want to take lessons from me?" Matsumura spoke only the truth; the engraver's reputation was high in both Naha and Shuri.

"Perhaps it isn't much of a reason," said the engraver, "but frankly I am curious to see how you yourself teach karate."

Was there some quality in the engraver's voice that annoyed the younger man? Was it the presumption that the teacher of the head of the clan might become the engraver's teacher? Ready, like many young men, to take offense, Matsumura cried angrily, "How pigheaded you are! How many times must it tell you—*I don't want to teach karate*!"

"Then," said the engraver, his tone of voice rather less

NO WEAPONS

polite than it had been in the beginning, "if you refuse to teach me, will you refuse also to grant me a match?"

"What is this?" asked Matsumura incredulously. "You want a match with me? With *me*?"

"Exactly! And why not? In a match there are no class distinctions. Furthermore, since you're no longer teaching the head of the clan, you don't need his permission to meet me in a match. And I can assure you I'll take better care of my legs and my shoulder than he did." By this time, the engraver's words, as well as his tone of voice, could only be regarded as insolent.

"I know you're said to be very good at karate," said Matsumura, "although of course I have no idea how good. But don't you think you may have gone too far? It wouldn't be a matter of being hurt or not; it would be a matter of life and death. Are you so set upon dying?"

"I'm quite willing to die," replied the engraver.

"Then I'll be happy to oblige you," said Matsumura. "No one, of course, can foresee the future, but there is an old saying: if two tigers fight, one is bound to be hurt and the other to die. So whether you win or lose, you may be sure you will not return home with an unscathed body. The time and place of our encounter," Matsumura concluded, "I leave up to you."

The engraver suggested five o'clock the following morning, and Matsumura concurred. The place agreed upon was the graveyard at Kinbu Palace, which lies behind Tama Palace.

Promptly at five o'clock the two men stood facing each other, a distance of some twelve yards between them. The engraver made the first move, closing the gap by about half, at which point he thrust out his left fist in a *gedan* position and held his right fist at his right hip. Matsumura, having risen from the rock on which he had been sitting, stood facing his opponent in a natural position (*shizen tai*), with his chin resting at his left shoulder.

Baffled by the posture his opponent had assumed, the engraver wondered if the man had taken leave of his senses. It was a fighting posture that seemed to offer no hope of defense, and the engraver prepared to launch his attack. Just at that very moment, Matsumura opened his eyes wide and looked deep into the eyes of the other. Repelled by a force that felt like a bolt of lightning, the engraver fell back. Matsumura had not moved a muscle; he stood where he had stood before, apparently defenseless.

Sweat beaded the engraver's brow, and his armpits were already damp; he could feel his heart beating with unaccustomed rapidity. He sat down on a nearby rock. Matsumura did the same. "What happened?" the engraver muttered to himself. "Why all this sweat? Why is my heart beating so wildly? We haven't yet exchanged a single blow!"

Then he heard Matsumura's voice: "Hey! Come on! The sun is rising. Let's get on with it!"

The two men rose, and Matsumura once again assumed the same natural position he had taken earlier. The engraver, for his part, was determined to complete the attack this time, and he advanced toward his opponent—from twelve yards to ten, then to eight . . . six . . . four. And there he stopped, unable to proceed any further, immobilized by the intangible force that flashed from Matsumura's eyes. His own eyes lost their luster, and he stood entranced by the radiance from Matsumura eyes.

At the same time, he was quite unable to tear his glance away from that of his opponent; in his bones he knew that if he did, something very terrible would happen.

How was he to extricate himself from this predicament? Suddenly he gave voice to a great shout, a *kiai*, which sounded like "Yach!" and boomed across the cemetery and echoed back from the surrounding hills. But Matsumura still stood unmoved. At this sight, the engraver once again sprang back startled and dismayed.

Master Matsumura smiled. "What's the matter?" he called. "Why don't you attack? You can't fight a match just by shouting!"

"I don't understand," the engraver replied. "I've never before lost a bout. And now . . ." After a moment's silence, he lifted his face and called quietly to Matsumura: "Yes, let's go on! The result of the match has already been decided, I know that, but let's finish it. If we don't, I'll lose face—and I'd rather be dead. I warn you, I'm going to attack in *sutemi*" (meaning he would fight to the finish).

"Good!" Matsumura called back. "Come on!"

"Then forgive me if you will," said the engraver as he launched his attack, but just then there issued from Matsumura's throat a great cry that sounded to the engraver like a thunderbolt. As the lightning of Matsumura's eyes had earlier immobilized him, so now did the thunder of Matsumura's voice. The engraver found he could not move; he made one last feeble attempt to attack before falling in a defeated heap to the ground. A few feet away, Matsumura's head was gilded by the rising sun: he seemed to the prostrate engraver like one of the ancient godly kings who slew demons and dragons.

"I give up!" cried the poor engraver. "I give up!"

"What!" cried Matsumura. "That's no way for an expert to talk!"

"I was a fool to challenge you," said the engraver, rising. "The result was obvious from the very beginning. I feel completely ashamed. There's just no comparison between my skill and yours."

"Not at all," replied Matsumura gently. "Your fighting spirit is excellent, and I suspect you have a great deal of skill. If we had actually fought, I might well have been defeated."

"You flatter me," said the engraver. "The fact is, I felt completely helpless when I looked at you. I was so frightened by your eyes that I lost whatever fighting spirit I had."

Matsumura's voice became soft. "Perhaps," he said. "But I know this: you were determined to win and I was just as determined to die if I lost. That was the difference between us.

"Listen," he went on. "When I came into your shop yesterday, I was very unhappy about being reprimanded by the head of the clan. When you challenged me, I was worried about that too, but once we decided on a match, all my worries suddenly vanished. I realized that I had been obsessed with relatively minor matters—with refinements of technique, with the skills of teaching, with flattering the head of the clan. I had been preoccupied with retaining my position.

"Today I'm a wiser man than I was yesterday. I'm a human being, and a human being is a vulnerable creature, who cannot possibly be perfect. After he dies, he returns to the elements—to earth, to water, to fire, to wind, to air. Matter is void. All is vanity. We are like blades of grass

28   NO WEAPONS

or trees of the forest, creations of the universe, of the spirit of the universe, and the spirit of the universe has neither life nor death. Vanity is the only obstacle to life."

With that, he fell silent. The engraver was silent too, pondering the invaluable lesson he had been taught. Whenever, in later years, he spoke about the incident to his friends, he never failed to describe his former opponent in the most glowing terms as a man of true greatness.

As for Matsumura, he was before long reappointed to his former position as personal instructor in karate to the head of the clan.

Unrecorded History

Inasmuch as there is virtually no written material on the early history of karate, we do not know who invented and developed it, nor even, for that matter, where it originated and evolved. Its earliest history may only be inferred from ancient legends that have been handed down to us by word of mouth, and they, like most legends, tend to be imaginative and probably inaccurate.

In my childhood, during the first years of Meiji, as I mentioned earlier, karate was banned by the government. It could not be practiced legally, and of course there were no karate dōjō. Nor were there any professional instructors. Men who were known to be adepts accepted a few pupils in secret, but their livelihood depended on work quite unrelated to karate. And those who succeeded in being taken on as students did so because of their interest in the art. At the very first, for example, I was Master Azato's only student and one of the very few who studied under Master Itosu.

There being no professional instructors, very little emphasis was placed on written descriptions of techniques and the like, a lack that a man like me, whose mission in life has been the propagation of Karate-dō, has regretted very deeply. Although I obviously cannot hope to remedy the lack, I shall attempt to set down what I remember hearing from my teachers about the legends that have survived in Okinawa. Alas, I know that my memory is not always reliable, and I am sure that I will make my share of errors. Nevertheless, I will do my best to note here what little I have learned about the origin and development of karate in Okinawa.

Napoleon is said to have observed that somewhere in the Far East there was a small kingdom whose people possessed not a single weapon. There seems little doubt that he was referring to the Ryukyu Islands, to what is now the prefecture of Okinawa, and that karate must have originated, developed, and become popular with the people of the islands for that very reason: because they were prohibited by law from bearing arms.

There were, in fact, two such prohibitive decrees: one promulgated about five centuries ago, the second some two hundred years later. Before the proclamation of the first decree, the Ryukyus were divided into three warring kingdoms: Chuzan, Nanzan and Hokuzan. It was the monarch of Chuzan, Shō Hashi, who, once he had succeeded in unifying the three kingdoms, issued a command prohibiting all Ryukyuans from possessing weapons, even rusty old swords. He also invited the famous scholars and statesmen of the three kingdoms to his capital city of Shuri, where he established a centralized government that was to endure for the next two centuries.

In the year 1609, however, the reigning king of the dynasty found himself obliged to outfit an army for the sake of repelling an invasion of the islands that had been launched by Shimazu, the daimyo of Satsuma (now Kagoshima Prefecture). The newly armed Ryukyuan warriors fought with conspicuous bravery and gallantry against the soldiers of the Satsuma clan, known and feared throughout the country for their fighting skill, but, after Ryukyuan success in a few pitched battles, a surprise landing by Shimazu's forces sealed the fate both of the islands and of their monarch, who was forced to surrender.

Since Shimazu reissued the edict banning weapons, many Ryukyuans (most of them members of the *shizoku* class) began secretly to practice a form of self-defense wherein hands and legs were the only weapons. What this actually was may only be conjectured. However, it is known that, for many centuries, Okinawa engaged in trade with the people of Fukien Province in southern China, and it was probably from this source that Chinese *kempo* ("boxing") was introduced into the islands.

It was from *kempo* that the present-day karate evolved. It was first known as "Okinawate," and I recall, when I was a child, hearing my elders speak of both "Okinawate" and "karate" (the *kara* in this case referring to China). I began then to think of Okinawate as an indigenous Okinawan fighting art and of karate as a Chinese form of boxing. In any case, I perceived a clear distinction between the two.

During the years of arms prohibition, inspectors were sent to the islands from Satsuma to ensure that the prohibition was being strictly observed, so it is hardly surprising that karate (which, as it developed, enabled a man to kill without weapons) could only be practiced and engaged in clandestinely. As I noted earlier, this clandestine aspect of karate persisted through the early years of Meiji, in part because the ancient decree lingered on in the minds of the people.

It is my own observation that Okinawan folk dances make use of a number of movements that are similar to those used in karate, and the reason, I believe, is that adepts who practiced the martial art in secret incorporated those movements into the dances in order to further confuse the authorities. Certainly anyone who carefully observes Okinawan folk dances (and they have today become quite popular in the large cities) will note that they differ markedly from the more graceful dances of the other Japanese islands. Okinawan dancers, male and female, use their hands and legs far more energetically, and their entrance onto the dancing area, as well as their departure from it, are also reminiscent of the beginning and end of any karate kata.

Indeed, the essence of the art has been summarized in the words: "Karate begins and ends with courtesy." As for Okinawa itself, its people for many, many centuries regarded their country as a place where all the forms of etiquette were most strictly observed.

The famous gate in front of Shuri Castle was called Shurei no Mon: "the Gate of Courtesy." After the Meiji government came to power and Okinawa became a prefecture, the Shurei no Mon, along with the castle to which it gave access, was designated a national treasure. Alas, the Shurei no Mon exists no more: it was totally destroyed during the battle for Okinawa toward the close of the Second World War. How ironic it is that American military bases now occupy the ground adjacent to that where once stood the gate that symbolized peace! [Since this was written, the Shurei no Mon has been reconstructed in its original form.]

Chinese Hand to Empty Hand

The Japanese language is not an easy one to master, nor is it always quite so explicit as it might be: different characters may have exactly the same pronunciation, and a single character may have different pronunciations, depending upon the use. The expression *karate* is an excellent example. *Te* is easy enough; it means "hand(s)." But there are two quite different characters that are both pronounced *kara*; one means "empty," and the other is the Chinese character referring to the Tang dynasty and may be translated "Chinese."

So should our martial art be written with the characters that mean "empty hand(s)" or with those that mean "Chinese hand(s)"? Here again we are in the shadowy realm of conjecture, but I believe I am safe in saying that before I came to Tokyo from Okinawa in the early 1920s, it was customary to use the character for "Chinese" rather than that for "empty" to write karate, but this certainly does not mean that the use of the "Chinese" *kara* was necessarily correct.

True, in Okinawa we used the word *karate*, but more often we called the art merely *te* or *bushi no te*, "warrior's hand(s)." Thus, we might speak of a man as having studied *te* or as having had experience in *bushi no te*. As to when *te* first became karate in Okinawan usage, I must refrain from offering even a conjecture, since there is no written material in existence that would provide us with the vaguest hint, much less tell us whether the character used was that for "Chinese" or that for "empty." Most probably, because Okinawa had long been under Chinese influence and because whatever was imported from China was considered to be both excellent and fashionable, it was the "Chinese" *kara* rather than the "empty" *kara*, but this, as I say, can only be the merest guesswork.

Actually, the two kinds of te taught and practiced in Okinawa might more correctly have been called *Shurite* and *Nawate*, after the two different schools of karate on the island. But the characters for "Chinese hand(s)" seem to have become the most popular, and, perhaps as a result, people came to believe that karate was actually a form of the Chinese boxing art. Even today there are those who hold that opinion, but in fact karate as practiced today is very different indeed from the ancient Chinese art of boxing.

Largely for that reason, I found it difficult to believe that "Chinese hand(s)" was the correct term to describe Okinawan karate as it has evolved over the centuries. Then, a few years after I came to Tokyo, I had an opportunity to express my disagreement with this traditional way of writing. It came about when Keio University formed a karate research group, and I was able then to suggest that the art be renamed *Dai Nippon Kempo Karate-dō* ("Great Japan Fist-Method Empty-Hands Way"), making use of the character for "empty" rather than that for "Chinese."

My suggestion initially elicited violent outbursts of criticism in both Tokyo and Okinawa, but I had confidence in the change and have adhered to it over the years. Since then, it has in fact gained such wide acceptance that the word *karate* would look strange to all of us now if it were written with the "Chinese" *kara* character.

The *kara* that means "empty" is definitely the more appropriate. For one thing, it symbolizes the obvious fact that this art of self-defense makes use of no weapons, only bare feet and empty hands. Further, students of Karate-dō aim not only toward perfecting their chosen art but also toward emptying heart and mind of all earthly desire and vanity. Reading Buddhist scriptures, we come across such statements as "Shiki-soku-ze-ku" and "Ku-soku-zeshiki," which literally mean, "matter is void" and "all is vanity." The character *ku*, which appears in both admonitions and may also be pronounced *kara*, is in itself truth.

Thus, although the martial arts are many and include such diverse forms as judo, fencing, archery, spear fighting and stick fighting, the ultimate objective of all of them is the same as that of karate. Believing with the Buddhists that it is emptiness, the void, that lies at the heart of all matter and indeed of all creation, I have steadfastly persisted in the use of that particular character in my naming of the martial art to which I have given my life. Indeed, I have much more to say on the use of *kara* meaning "empty," but as space is limited and these philosophical problems have little place here, I shall refrain from going into the problem any more deeply. And the subject is dealt with in greater detail in another of my books, *Karate-dō Kyōhan: The Master Text*.

Once I realized that I was destined to succeed in popularizing the change from "Chinese" hands to "empty" hands, I embarked upon other tasks of revision and simplification. Hoping to see karate included in the universal physical education taught in our public schools, I set about revising the kata so as to make them as simple as possible. Times change, the world changes, and obviously the martial arts must change too. The karate that high school students practice today is not the same karate that was practiced even as recently as ten years ago, and it is a long way indeed from the karate that I learned when I was a child in Okinawa.

Inasmuch as there are not now, and never have been, any hard and fast rules regarding the various kata, it is hardly surprising to find that they change not only with the times but also from instructor to instructor. What is most important is that karate, as a form of sport used in physical education, should be simple enough to be practiced without undue difficulty by everybody, young and old, boys and girls, men and women.

Another reform to which I gave my attention was that of nomenclature. Shortly after I came to Tokyo in 1922, the firm of Bukyosha published a book I had written called *Ryūkyū Kempo: Karate*. At that time, the word was still being written as "Chinese hands," and almost all the names of the kata that I described in my book were of Okinawan origin: Pinan, Naifanchi, Chinto, Bassai, Seishan, Jitte, Jion, Sanchin, and the like. These were, in fact, the names that I had learned long ago from my own teachers.

No one, by now, had any idea how they had come into being, and people found them difficult to learn. Accordingly, after having transformed "Chinese hands" into "empty hands," I began to give the kata names that were easier for the Japanese people to use and that have now become familiar all over the world: Ten no Kata, Chi no

Kata, Hito no Kata, Empi, Gankaku, Hangetsu, Meikyō, Hakkō, Kiun, Shōtō, Shōin, Hotaku, Shōkyō and so on. Let me hasten to assure the reader that I labor under no misapprehension that the names I have chosen are changeless and eternal. I have no doubt whatsoever that in the future, as times change, again and then again, the kata will be given new names. And that, indeed, is as it should be.

Karate-dō Is One

One serious problem, in my opinion, which besets present-day Karate-dō is the prevalence of divergent schools. I believe that this will have a deleterious effect on the future development of the art.

In Okinawa in older times there were, as we know, two schools, Nawate and Shurite, and these were thought of as being related to the two schools of Chinese boxing called Wutang and Shorinji Kempo that flourished during the Yuan, Ming and Chin dynasties. The founding of the Wutang school is attributed to a certain Chang San-feng, while the founder of the Shorinji school was said to have been Daruma himself (Bodhidharma), the founder of Zen Buddhism. Both schools, according to report, were extremely popular, and their adherents gave frequent public demonstrations.

Legend tells us that the Wutang school got its name from the Chinese mountain on which it was said to have first been practiced, while Shorinji is the Japanese pronunciation for the Shaolin Temple in Hunan Province, where Daruma preached the way of the Buddha. According to one version of the story, his followers were physically unequal to the rigors of the training he demanded, and after many had fallen in exhaustion, he ordered them to begin, the very next morning, to train their bodies so that their minds and hearts would grow to accept and follow the way of the Buddha. His method of training was a form of boxing that came to be known as Shorinji Kempo. However much of the legends we accept as historical fact, I think there is little doubt that Chinese boxing did indeed cross the sea to Okinawa, where it merged with an indigenous Okinawan style of fist fighting to form the basis of what we now know as karate.

Formerly, the two Chinese schools of boxing were associated with two Okinawan schools, Shōrin-ryū and Shōrei-ryū, but what precise relationship existed among them is, of course, long lost in the mists of time. The same is true, incidentally, of the Shurite and the Nawate schools.

What we do know is that the techniques of the Shōrei school were best suited to a person with a large body, while Shōrin techniques suited people with a smaller frame and less strength. Both schools had their advantages and disadvantages. Shōrei, for example, taught a more effective form of self-defense, but it lacked the mobility of Shōrin. Karate techniques of the present day have adopted the best qualities of both schools.

Again I say that this is as it should be. There is no place in contemporary Karate-dō for different schools. Some instructors, I know, claim to have invented new and unusual kata, and so they arrogate to themselves the right to be called founders of "schools." Indeed, I have heard myself and my colleagues referred to as the Shōtō-kan school, but I strongly object to this attempt at classification. My belief is that all these "schools" should be amalgamated into one so that Karate-dō may pursue an orderly and useful progress into man's future.

My Wife's Karate

I have already mentioned the fact that my family came from the shizoku class. My paternal grandfather, Gifuku, became a noted Confucian scholar, and like most scholars he had few money worries—that is, he had very little money to worry about. He was, however, in high favor with the *hanshu* ("head of the clan") and was given the duty and the honor of instructing the *hanshu*'s widowed daughters in Confucian ethics. These private lessons took place at the Kuntoku Daikun Goten, a palace where the ladies lived and where there was also, incidentally, a shrine dedicated to the ancestors of the *hanshu*. Men were, of course, forbidden to enter the ladies' palace, but an exception was made for Gifuku.

After he had grown too old to go on teaching, he resigned his post and was rewarded by the hanshu with a house in Teira-machi, near the palace; at the time of the Meiji Restoration, he was also given quite a substantial sum of money. Unhappily, after my grandfather's death, all the property and all the money that he bequeathed my father were slowly but surely dissipated.

Unlike me, my father was tall and handsome. He was expert at stick fighting (*bōjitsu*), and an accomplished singer and dancer, but he possessed one unfortunate defect. He was a heavy drinker, and that, I suspect, is how and why Gifuku's legacy gradually made its way out of our family's hands. The house we lived in, even when I was a child, was always a rented one.

Because of our relative poverty, I did not marry until I was over twenty—quite an advanced age for marriage in those days in Okinawa. My salary as a primary schoolteacher was the princely sum of three yen a month, and on that amount I had to support not only my wife and myself but also my parents and grandparents; nor were schoolteachers permitted to do any sort of extra remunerative work. Further, I was working very hard at karate, which however much I loved it, brought in not a single sen.

So there we were, a family of ten, subsisting on an income of three yen a month. The fact that we were able to do so was due entirely to the diligence of my wife. Late into the night, for example, she would be hard at work weaving a local cloth called *kasuri*, for which she would be paid six sen a bolt. Then she would rise with the dawn and walk well over a mile to a small field where she grew the family's vegetables. Sometimes I would accompany her, but in those days it was considered most improper for a schoolteacher to be seen working in the fields beside his wife. So I could not go with her very often, and when I did, I wore a large, wide-brimmed hat to keep from being recognized.

I used to wonder when she found time to sleep, but not once can I recall ever hearing a word of complaint from her. Nor did she ever suggest that I might spend my time more profitably than practicing karate every free minute I had. On the contrary, she encouraged me to continue with it, and she herself took an interest in it, frequently watching my practice sessions. And when she felt particularly weary, she did not, as most women would have done, lie down and ask one of the children to massage her

NO WEAPONS

shoulders and arms. Oh no, not my wife! What she did to relieve her exhausted body was go outside and practice karate kata, and in due course she became so adept that her movements were as dextrous as those of an expert.

On the days that I did not practice under the sharp eyes of Azato or Itosu, I would practice by myself in our yard. Several young men of the neighborhood, who had been watching me, came to me one day and asked me to teach them karate, which I was of course very glad to do. Sometimes, however, I would be delayed at school, and on those occasions I would return home to find the young men practicing by themselves, with my wife encouraging them and correcting them when they did anything wrong. Merely by watching me practice, and by practicing occasionally herself, she had attained a full understanding of the art.

For our house we paid a monthly rent of twenty-five sen, which was quite a large sum in those days. Our neighbors were mostly small tradesmen or jinriksha men. Some sold house slippers, some articles like combs, some the bean curd we call *tofu*. In any case, our neighbors would frequently grow quarrelsome after they had been drinking.

At such times it would usually be my wife who would intercede and make peace. This she almost always succeeded in doing even after the quarrel had degenerated into a fistfight—not an easy task even for a strong man. Of course she did not use violence in her role as mediator; she depended entirely on her powers of persuasion. Thus, my wife, admired at home for her diligence and thrift, was known throughout the neighborhood as a karate adept and a skillful mediator.

End of Secrecy

It was in the first or second year of the present century, as I recall, that our school was visited by Shintarō Ogawa, who was then commissioner of schools for Kagoshima Prefecture. Among the various exhibitions that had been arranged for him was a demonstration of karate. He seemed greatly impressed by it, but only later did I learn that upon his return from Okinawa he submitted a detailed report to the Ministry of Education, greatly extolling the virtues of the art. As a result of Ogawa's report, karate became part of the curriculum of the Prefectural Daiichi Middle School and the Men's Normal School. The martial art that I had studied in secret when I was very poor had at last emerged from seclusion and had even won the approval of the Ministry of Education. I did not know how to express my deep gratitude to Ogawa, but I determined to devote all the time and effort I could spare to the popularization of the art.

Once the decision had been made to include karate in school curriculums, it began to exert its inevitable appeal on all sorts of people. Not only middle schools but also youth organizations and even primary schools adopted this subtle art of self-defense as one of their physical education courses, and many people came to me for advice and instruction. After I had secured the permission of both Azato and Itosu, I announced that I would take students on a formal basis, and I can still recall the spark of joy I felt when I stood before my first karate class.

Some years after that, Admiral Rokurō Yashiro (who was then a captain) brought his training vessel into a nearby port, and one day during his visit he came to view a performance of karate kata given by my primary school pupils. So impressed was he that he at once issued orders to the officers and men in his command to come to see our demonstrations and then to set about learning the art. This was, I believe, the first time that navy men had ever witnessed a karate performance.

Then, in 1912, the Imperial Navy's First Fleet, which was under the command of Admiral Dewa, anchored in Chūjo Bay, and a dozen members of the ships' crews stayed for a week in the dormitory of the Prefectural Daiichi Middle School in order to observe and practice karate. Thus, thanks to the enthusiasm of Captain Yashiro and Admiral Dewa, karate came to be talked about in Tokyo, but very little was actually known about it as yet. Not, as I recall, until another ten years had elapsed did karate men from Okinawa go to Tokyo to introduce and teach the art.

In 1921 the crown prince (now the emperor) called at Okinawa while en route to Europe. Captain Norikazu Kanna, who was in command of the destroyer on which the prince was traveling, was an Okinawan by birth, and I believe it was he who originally made the suggestion that the prince observe a karate demonstration. This was arranged, and I was granted the honor of taking charge of the demonstration, held in the Great Hall of Shuri Castle. Many years have passed since that day, but I still recall vividly how thrilled I felt. Later I was told that the prince said he had been much impressed by three things in Okinawa: the lovely scenery, the Dragon Drain of the Magic Fountain in Shuri Castle and karate.

It was shortly before the prince's visit to Okinawa that

I resigned my job as a schoolteacher. Strangely enough, it was a promotion that caused my resignation, for I was ordered by my superiors to go to an outlying island in the archipelago, where I was to be the principal of the primary school. My mother, however, was old and bedridden, and I, her only son, did not feel I could leave her, so I had no alternative but to tender my resignation. Some three decades of life as a schoolteacher had come to an end, but I am happy to report that I did not altogether sever my connections with the Okinawan school system. After consulting with Shoko Makaina, the head of the Okinawa Prefectural Library, and Bakumonto Sueyoshi, the managing editor of the *Okinawa Times*, I organized the Okinawa Students Supporting Society and later became its director. At the same time, I also established with the help of my colleagues another group, the Okinawa Association for the Spirit of the Martial Arts, to further the unification of Karate-dō.

TRAINING FOR LIFE

Against a Typhoon

Perhaps it would be more modest to let another person describe one's youthful feats than to do so oneself. But resolutely swallowing my sense of shame, I shall here quote the words of Yukio Togawa, the author, taking no responsibility for them beyond assuring my readers that the incident described is a true one. The reader may see a touch of madness, but I have no regrets.

"The sky above," writes Mr. Togawa, "was black, and out of it there came a howling wind that laid waste to whatever stood in its path. Huge branches were torn like twigs from great trees, and dust and pebbles flew through the air, stinging a man's face.

"Okinawa is known as the island of typhoons, and the ferocity of its tropical storms defies description. To withstand the onslaught of the winds that devastate the island regularly every year during the storm season, the houses of Okinawa stand low and are built as sturdily as possible; they are surrounded by high stone walls, and the slate tiles on the roofs are secured by mortar. But the winds are so tremendous (sometimes attaining a velocity of one hundred miles per hour) that despite all precautions the houses shiver and tremble.

"During one particular typhoon that I remember, all the people of Shuri huddled together within their homes, praying for the typhoon to pass without wreaking any great damage. No, I was wrong when I said all the people of Shuri huddled at home: there was one young man, up on the roof of his house in Yamakawa-chō, who was determinedly battling the typhoon.

"Anyone observing this solitary figure would surely have concluded that he had lost his wits. Wearing only a loincloth, he stood on the slippery tiles of the roof and held in both hands, as though to protect him from the howling wind, a tatami mat. He must have fallen off the roof to the ground time and again, for his nearly naked body was smeared all over with mud.

"The young man seemed to be about twenty years old, or perhaps even younger. He was of small stature, hardly more than five feet tall, but his shoulders were huge and his biceps bulged. His hair was dressed like that of a sumō wrestler, with a topknot and a small silver pin, indicating that he belonged to the shizoku.

"But all this is of little importance. What matters is the expression on his face: wide eyes glittering with a strange light, a wide brow, copper red skin. Clenching his teeth as the wind tore at him, he gave off an aura of tremendous power. One might have said he was one of the guardian Deva kings.

"Now the young man on the roof assumed a low posture, holding the straw mat aloft against the raging wind. The stance he took was most impressive, for he stood as if astride a horse. Indeed, anyone who knew karate could readily have seen that the youth was taking the horse-riding stance, the most stable of all karate stances, and that he was making use of the howling typhoon to refine his technique and to further strengthen both body and mind. The wind struck the mat and the youth with full force, but he stood his ground and did not flinch."

Meeting with a Viper

In Okinawa, there is a very poisonous pit viper called *habu*. Happily, its bite is no longer quite the fearsome thing that it was in my younger days when, if a person was bitten on hand or foot, the only way to save his life was immediate amputation. Now an effective serum has been developed, but it must be injected as soon as possible after the bite. Our Okinawan *habu*, which grows to a length of six or seven feet, is still a good beast to avoid.

Back in the old days before the development of the serum, I went one night to the house of Master Azato for a karate practice session. This occurred several years after my marriage, and I asked my eldest son, then in primary school, to accompany me and carry the little lantern that lighted our way through the island night.

As we were walking through Sakashita, between Naha and Shuri, we passed an old temple dedicated to the ancient and much venerated Goddess of Mercy, called Kannon in modern Japanese. Just after we passed her temple I spied in the middle of the road an object that I first took to be horse droppings, but as we drew nearer I realized that what I was looking at was alive—and not only alive but coiled to strike, glaring angrily at the two intruders.

When my young son saw those two piercing eyes glittering in the night and then, by the light of the lantern, that sharp red tongue darting out, he shrieked in terror and threw himself upon me, clutching my thighs in his fear. I quickly thrust him behind me, grabbed the lantern from him, and began to swing it slowly from right to left, keeping my own eyes riveted to those of the viper. I cannot, of course, say how long this went on, but at last the snake, still glaring at me, slithered off into the darkness of a nearby potato field. It was only then that I could see how very long and thick that habu was.

I had, naturally, often seen habu before, but never until that night had I seen one coiled to strike. Knowing, as every Okinawan does, their unpleasant habits, I very much doubted that it would slither off quite so submissively without making even an attempt to attack, so—terribly frightened though I was—I held the lantern in front of me as I crept into the field in search of the snake.

I soon saw those two glistening eyes reflected in the light of the lantern and realized that the habu was indeed expecting me. It had set its trap and was now waiting for me to spring it. Fortunately, seeing me and seeing that swinging lantern, the snake abandoned his attack and this time disappeared for good into the darkness of the field.

It seemed to me that I had learned an important lesson from that viper. As we continued on our way toward Azato's house, I said to my son, "We all know about the habu's persistence. But this time that was not the danger. The habu we encountered appears to be familiar with the tactics of karate, and when it slid off into the field it was not running away from us. It was preparing for an attack. That habu understands very well the spirit of karate."

Win by Losing

I should like to recount two incidents that may, I think, help my readers to understand the essence of Karate-dō.

Both incidents occurred many years ago in the Okinawan countryside, and both illustrate how a man may win by losing.

The first took place on a road southwest of Shuri Castle that led to a former governor's villa called Ochaya Goten. Within the compound of the villa stood a teahouse built after the ancient Nara fashion, with a commanding view over the Pacific. The governor, after days of hard work, would come here to relax with his wife and children.

The distance from Shuri was a little over a mile, and the road was paved with stone and lined on both sides by tall and stately pine trees. After the villa, no longer the private property of the governor, was opened to the public, I went there one evening with Master Itosu and half a dozen other karateka for a moon-viewing party. Our group being a congenial one, we lost track of the time and stayed on until quite late, talking about karate and reciting poetry.

Finally we decided that it was indeed time to go home and set out along the tree-lined road to Shuri. The moon was now veiled by a thick mist, and the younger men carried lanterns to help light the way for the teacher. Suddenly the man who was leading the party shouted that we should all douse our lanterns. We did so, only to learn that we were about to be attacked. The number of our assailants seemed to be about the same as the number of our party, so from that point of view we were evenly matched, but unless our assailants were also karate adepts they were doomed to ignominious defeat. It was so dark that we could not see anyone's face.

I turned to Itosu for instructions, but all he said was, "Stand with your backs to the moon! Your backs to the moon!" I was quite surprised, for I had thought that surely our teacher would now give us a chance to practice our karate and of course all of us were more than ready to take on this gang of thugs. But Itosu told us merely to turn our backs to the moon! It seemed to make no sense.

After a few minutes, he whispered into my ear, "Funakoshi, why don't you go and have a talk with them? They may not be bad men at heart. And if you tell them I'm a member of the party, that might make all the difference."

I acknowledged the instruction and started walking toward the waiting gang. "One of them's coming!" I heard someone cry. "One of them's coming! Get ready!" The atmosphere now seemed but a moment away from the start of a battle royal.

As I approached them I could see that our would-be assailants had all covered their faces with towels, so that it would be impossible to identify them. As instructed, I told them politely that Master Itosu was one of our group and that we were all his students. "Perhaps," I added quietly, "this is a case of mistaken identity."

"Itosu? Who's he?" muttered one of the gang. "Never heard of him!"

Another, seeing how short I was, cried, "Hey, you're just a kid! What are you doing—sticking your nose into men's affairs? Just get out of the way!" And with that, he started to grab me by the chest.

I lowered my hips into a karate stance. But at that moment I heard Itosu's voice: "No fighting, Funakoshi! Listen to what they have to say. Talk to them."

"Well," I addressed the men, "what is it you've got against us? Let's hear it!"

Before anyone had a chance to reply, we were joined by

a group of men who had obviously had quite a bit to drink and who were now singing boisterously as they made their way home. When they got close enough to realize that there was a confrontation in progress, they began to shout happily at the prospect of seeing a good bloody fight. But then one of them recognized our leader.

"You're Master Itosu!" he cried. "Aren't you? Of course you are! What on earth's the matter?" Then he turned to the gang that wanted to attack us. "What, are you guys crazy?" he said. "Don't you know who these people are? That's Itosu, the karate master, with his students. Ten or even twenty of you couldn't beat them in a free-for-all. You'd better apologize, and you'd better be quick about it!"

There was, in fact, no apology, but the gang of men muttered among themselves for a moment, after which they quietly faded away into the night. Then Itosu issued another instruction that we all found rather mysterious. Instead of continuing on the way we had started, he ordered us to retrace our steps and take a longer road back to Shuri. Until we reached his house, he did not say a word about the encounter; then he made us all promise not to speak about it. "You've done a good job tonight, boys," he said. "I have no doubt you'll become first-rate karateka. But don't say a word about what happened tonight to anyone! Not to anyone, do you understand?"

Later I learned that the members of the gang had come rather shamefacedly to Itosu's house in order to apologize. It turned out that the men we had thought to be thugs or thieves were in fact *sanka*—that is, men who worked in a village where the very potent Okinawan liquor called *awamori* is distilled. They were merely rather rowdy, rough-and-tumble citizens, proud of their physical strength, who had chosen us that night as suitable material upon which to test their prowess. It was only then that I realized how clever the master had been to order us to return to Shuri by a different route so as to avoid any further encounters. Therein, I thought, lies the meaning of karate. My cheeks grew hot and red as I realized that but for Itosu I would have used my skill and my strength against untrained men.

The second incident, which is of a somewhat similar nature, has a more satisfactory ending. First, however, I must say a word about my wife's family. For many years they had been experimenting with the sweet potato plant, trying to evolve an improved strain. They had been moderately prosperous but with the Meiji Restoration of 1868 had fallen on hard times and moved to a small farming village, called Mawashi, about two and a half miles from Naha. My wife's father, a staunch adherent of the Obstinate Party, had become something of an eccentric. When the weather was fine, he tended his fields; when it rained, he stayed home and read; and that was all he did.

My wife was very fond of him, and one festival day she went early with the children in order to have a nice long visit. Late that afternoon, I myself started off for the village, as I did not like the idea of my wife and children walking home alone in the dark.

The lonely road to Mawashi wandered through thick pine groves, and in the fading afternoon light was quite dark, so I was taken quite by surprise when two men suddenly sprang from the shelter of the trees into the path to bar my way. Like the other would-be attackers, they had covered their faces with towels. It was evident at once that they were not merely bent on provoking a good-natured free-for-all.

"Well," cried one of them, in a most insolent tone, "don't just stand there as if you were deaf and dumb. You know what we want. Speak up! Say, 'Good evening, sir,' and tell us what a fine day it is. Don't waste our time, small-fry, or you'll be sorry. I can promise you that!"

The angrier they grew, the calmer I felt. I could tell from the way the one who had spoken to me clenched his fists that he was not a karate man; and the other, who was carrying a heavy stick, was also clearly an amateur. "Haven't you mistaken me," I asked quietly, "for someone else? Surely there has been some misunderstanding. I think if we talked it over . . ."

"Ah, shut up, you little shrimp!" snarled the man with the club. "What do you take us for?"

With this, the two moved a little nearer, but I did not feel intimidated in the least. "It seems," I said, "as though I'm going to have to fight you after all, but frankly my advice to you is not to insist. I don't think it's going to do you very much good because . . ."

The second of the two men now raised the heavy stick he was carrying.

". . . because," I went on quickly, "If I wasn't sure of winning, I wouldn't fight. I know I'm bound to lose. So why fight? Doesn't that make sense?"

At these words, the two seemed to calm down a bit. "Well," said one of them, "you certainly don't put up much of a fight. Let's have your money then."

"I haven't got any," I replied, showing them my empty pockets.

"Some tobacco then!"

"I don't smoke."

All that I did have, in fact, were some *manju*, cakes that I was taking to offer at the altar in the house of my wife's father. "Here," I said to the men, "take these."

"Only *manju*!" Their tone was disparaging. "Well, better than nothing." Taking the cakes, one of the men said, "Better get going, shrimp. And be careful, this path's kind of dangerous." With that, they disappeared into the trees.

A few days later I happened to be with both Azato and Itosu, and in the course of our conversation I told them about the incident. The first to praise me was Itosu, who said that I had behaved with the utmost propriety and that he now considered that the hours he had spent teaching me karate had been well-spent.

"But," asked Azato, smiling, "as you no longer had any *manju*, what did you offer at your father-in-law's altar?"

"Since I had nothing else," I replied, "I offered a heartfelt prayer."

"Ah, good, good!" cried Azato. "Well done, indeed! That's the true spirit of karate. Now you are beginning to understand what it means."

I tried to smother my pride. Although the two masters had never praised a single kata that I executed during our practice sessions, they were praising me now, and mingled with the pride was an abiding sense of joy.

The Danger of Pride

One evening, when I was just past my thirtieth birthday, I was walking from Naha back to Shuri. The road was a lonely one and grew lonelier after Sogenji temple. Along

54

the left stretched a graveyard, and nearby stood a large pond where in days long past warriors used to water their horses. Beside the pond was a grassy plot with a small stone platform in the center; here the youths of Okinawa came to test their strength in bouts of hand wrestling. That particular evening, as I passed, several young men were engaged in the sport.

As I have noted earlier, Okinawan hand wrestling is somewhat different from that practiced in the rest of Japan. I was very fond of the sport and (I must confess) felt no lack of confidence. I stood and watched for a time.

Then suddenly one of them shouted at me, "Hey, you! Come on and have a try! Unless of course you're afraid."

"Right!" cried another. "Don't just stand there watching. That's not very polite!"

I was really not looking for trouble, so I said, "Please excuse me, but I must go now," and started on my way.

"Oh no, you don't!" With that, a couple of the youths ran up to me.

"Running away?" taunted one.

"Don't you have any manners?" asked the other.

Together, the two had grabbed hold of my shirt and dragged me toward the stone platform. There sat an older man whom I took to be the referee—and probably the strongest hand wrestler in the group. No doubt I could have used the skills I had acquired and made a painless escape, but instead I decided to join the sport. My first bout, with the weakest looking of the lot, I won with ease. The second youth was also an easy victim. And so was the third, the fourth and the fifth.

Now there were only two men, one of them the referee, and both looked like strong opponents.

"Well," said the referee, with a nod to the other, "it's your turn now. Are you ready for a match with this stranger?"

"I'm afraid I'm not," I interposed. "I've had enough, and I'm sure I can't win anyway. Please excuse me."

But they were insistent. My next opponent, with a scowl, grabbed my hand, so I had no choice but to give battle. This bout, too, was mine, and in short order. "Now really I must go," I said. "Thank you. Please excuse me."

This time, apparently, my excuses were accepted. But as I started off toward Shuri, I had a feeling that the journey was not to be without incident. And I was right, for before very long I heard sounds behind me.

Luckily for me, when I left earlier in the day for Naha, I had an umbrella with me, for it had been raining. Now that the rain had ceased, I was using the umbrella as a walking stick; it would serve also, I decided, as a means of defense, so I quickly opened it and held it over the back of my head to ward off a blow from behind.

Well, I shall not make a long story of this. Although there must have been seven or eight in the group, I succeeded in evading all the blows that were aimed at me, until at last I heard the voice of the older man saying, "Who is this guy? He seems to know karate."

The attack ceased. The men stood around, glaring at me angrily, but there were no more blows, nor was any attempt made to stop me as I started on my way again. While I walked, I recited to myself one of my favorite poems and at the same time listened for sounds of stealthy movement but heard none.

By the time I reached Shuri, I was filled with remorse. Why had I entered that hand-wrestling competition? Was

56   TRAINING FOR LIFE

it, I asked myself, mere curiosity? But the real answer came to my mind: it was overconfidence in my strength. It was, in a word, pride. It was a violation of the spirit of Karate-dō, and I felt ashamed. Even as I tell the story now, these many years later, I still feel deeply ashamed.

Kindness without Pity

Near my grandfather's house, on a high hill, stood a thick forest called Bengadake. In it, there nestled a shrine reputed to ensure good fortune to those who came to worship there (of whom there were many from both Naha and Shuri). The forest itself was visible to voyagers entering Chūjo Bay.

One evening, walking from the village of Nishihara, I had almost reached the summit of the wooded hill of Bengadake when I suddenly perceived a man running toward me at full tilt. Had I not turned quickly aside, we would have had a head-on collision, and although by then it was quite dark, I realized from the man's movements that he had no knowledge of the art of self-defense.

After he plunged into a field of sugarcane, the high stalks hid him completely from sight. Since there was no longer any sound from the cane field, I feared that he might have stumbled, struck his head against a stone, and lost consciousness. However, although I searched the field as thoroughly as I could in the darkness, I could find no trace of him. How strange, I thought as I continued downward in the direction of a little hollow in which there was a community cesspool.

The stench was quite disgusting, and I would have gone on as quickly as possible had I not suddenly seen something floating in the muck that looked like a dark-colored melon. The object was—there could be no doubt of it—the head of a man, almost certainly the head of the man who had come hurtling down the hill. Despite the stench, I gave him a hand to help him out of the filth. Without even a word of thanks, he plunged on down the hill as fast as he could.

Just at that very moment, from the opposite direction, there came the blast of a whistle, and three black-cloaked figures loomed up in the darkness. Before I could utter a word, they had seized me. "Wait!" I cried, "you've got the wrong man," for by this time it was evident that the three were police officers. Saying that they were indeed policemen, they produced some rope to tie me up. It occurred to me then that they were after the man who had fallen into the muck.

"Hold on a minute," I repeated. "You've made a mistake."

"Don't lie to us," said one of the officers brusquely. "And don't make any more trouble."

The three seemed quite sure that I was the man they were searching for, but I persisted in my denials. Patiently I explained that their quarry had, only a few moments before, fallen into the cesspool and had then fled after I helped him out.

They were, at first, quite incredulous, but after another repetition of my story they began to believe me. Then they asked me how old the man was and what he looked like. I replied that it was far too dark for a man's eyes to be reliable witnesses but in view of what had happened no one's nose could possibly be mistaken about his identity.

At that, the four of us sped down the hill in the direction

the man had taken. When we reached the foot of the hill, we heard a man shout that he had found someone lying flat on his face on the ground. It now turned out that there was another group of policemen seeking the same culprit, who was found lying in the midst of a potato field. He was, or seemed to be, unconscious, and he stank to high heaven. There was no doubt that he was the man all these police officers were after.

They were about to tie him up and cart him off when I suggested they might at least clean him off a bit first.

"Well, where?" asked one of them in a surly voice.

"Bring him to my house," I said. "It's on the way to the police station anyway."

And that is what we did. We stripped him of his filthy clothes and washed him beside my well, and there I was astonished to see what had happened to him. From his right thigh ran a stream of blood, while his left thigh was black and blue. Evidently, he had been injured when he fell into the cesspool, and the painful bruise was apparently the result of the unintended kick I had given him when I wheeled to avoid him as he hurtled down the hill.

I felt a deep sense of pity for him, until the officers told me that he was an escaped convict with a long police record and that he had been convicted of theft, robbery and rape. Then my sense of pity vanished.

Mediation

In the northern part of the island of Okinawa, in the county of Kokuryo, there lies a coastal village named Motobe, and near it, also on the coast, stands a hamlet known as Shaka. Now Shaka, after the Meiji Restoration, was settled by Okinawan gentry dissatisfied with the new regime in Tokyo, and Shaka was the chief source of the nearly endless disputes that seemed to rock the county of Kokuryo year after year.

The incident I am about to recount occurred some fifteen years after I had started teaching, and it concerned a dispute that had arisen between Shaka and a neighboring hamlet. The local police found themselves unequal to settling the argument, which, as it showed no signs of abating, they referred to the police in Naha. However, since the origin of the dispute was political in nature, members of the county council, the prefectural council and the prefectural government itself were also called in to help. Strangely enough, I also was asked to join the arbitrating party. I had then, and have now, no idea why.

I was a member of the faculty of a small school near the bay of Senno in Chūto County, and for some time I had been hoping for a transfer to a school in the center of Naha, which would be more convenient for my karate practice, but the transfer had not come through. I wondered, in fact, if it was because of my knowledge of karate that I had been so eagerly solicited to become one of the arbitrators—not, to be sure, that I would be expected to settle the dispute in hand-to-hand combat but rather because many of the disputants would be karate adepts and might take kindly to my presence.

In any case, I felt I could not refuse, so I requested a brief leave of absence from the principal of my school. It was granted. There were, of course, no horseless carriages in Okinawa in those days, so off we started, early one morning, in horse-drawn buggies. As the distance between

Naha and Shaka was about fifty miles, we had to change horses twice, as I recall.

We arrived to find an atmosphere of strong suspicion and hostility between the two tiny hamlets, an atmosphere that we very much feared could only grow more belligerent until it burst into an outright battle. We resolved to exercise the utmost tact in an effort to keep matters well under control.

Then a very strange thing happened. The inhabitants of the two villages were gathered on neutral ground, angrily facing each other, with us in between, when suddenly, and almost simultaneously, out of the two opposing groups came a man from each to greet me in almost identical words. "Funakoshi," I heard them say, "whatever brings you here?"

Seeing me thus greeted, my fellow arbitrators asked me to try settling the dispute single-handedly. No doubt they thought that since I had a friend in each hamlet, I would be able to put an end to the argument easily and quickly, but I, for my part, felt far less optimistic and knew that a wrong word could lead to flying fists, which would push ultimate peace that much further away.

However, I agreed to take on the job. I decided to be as courteous and as impartial as was humanly possible, listening carefully to the arguments of both sides. This I did, but there were moments during that day and the next when it looked as though I was about to be attacked by crowds of angry villagers, first from one hamlet, then from the other. However, I kept my head and my patience and did nothing rash, and the threatened violence failed to materialize. Finally, after two days of careful listening, I proposed a compromise solution that turned out to be acceptable to both sides. With peace now concluded, a formal ceremony to celebrate the happy event was held at the Shaka primary school. Then the arbitrators climbed back into their buggies and returned to Naha.

A month later, I was called to the Educational Affairs Section of the Okinawa prefectural government, where I was informed that I had been promoted to a school in central Naha. What I had so dearly longed for had finally come to pass, and I could only attribute it to my training in karate, which had proved so useful in my mediation efforts.

A Humble Man

When I was still an assistant teacher at a school in Naha, I had a two-and-a-half mile walk twice a day, since my wife and I were living at that time at her parents' house in Shuri. One day there was a teachers' meeting that lasted quite a long time, so it was late when I started home, and it soon began to rain. I decided to be extravagant for once and hire a jinriksha.

To while away the time, I began a conversation with the jinriksha man and found, rather to my surprise, that he gave extremely short answers to my questions. Usually jinriksha men are as loquacious as barbers. Further, his tone of voice was extremely polite and his language was that of a well-educated man. Now in Okinawa at that time there were two kinds of jinrikshas: *hiruguruma* ("day jinrikshas") and *yoruguruma* ("night jinrikshas"), and I knew quite well that some of the night jinriksha men were gentry who had come down in the world.

Could this man, I wondered, who was pulling me along

to Shuri be someone I knew? If so, the proprieties would be offended. However, there remained the question of finding out, and that was not easy, for the man wore a wide-brimmed hat, with which he managed to keep his face concealed from me.

Accordingly, I devised a stratagem that I thought would permit me to see who he was. I asked him to stop the jinriksha for a moment so that I might answer a call of nature. As he laid the shafts down onto the ground, I got the distinct impression that this was no ordinary jinriksha man, but when, as I climbed down, I tried to take a peek at his face, he quickly turned his head away. Yet there was something naggingly familiar about the carriage of his tall, slender body.

By then the rain had stopped, and a pale moon had emerged from the clouds. After I had relieved myself, I returned to the jinriksha and again tried to have a look at the man's face and was again thwarted. Rather disgusted at my own incompetence, I hit upon another plan that I was convinced would work. "We've come quite a distance already," I said, "and you must be tired. It's a pleasant evening; why don't we walk for a bit?"

The man agreed, but here again I was unsuccessful, for he refused to walk by my side. He was always a pace or two behind. Suddenly, at a bend in the road, I wheeled around and grabbed a shaft of the jinriksha and at the same time tried to get a glimpse of his features. However, quick as I was, the man was even quicker, as he pulled his hat down deep over his face. So quick, indeed, was his reaction that I was now perfectly convinced he could not be an ordinary jinriksha man.

In fact, I was pretty sure I knew who he was. I took

off my hat and said, "Forgive me for asking, but aren't you Mr. Sueyoshi?"

Startled, he nonetheless answered firmly, "I am not."

So we stood for a moment as though in a tableau, I holding onto the jinriksha, he staring down at the ground, his face hidden by his wide hat. Then suddenly he came to a decision, took off his hat, and dropped to his knees. I saw that I was not mistaken. He was indeed Sueyoshi. I took him by the hand to help him up, and then I dropped to my knees as I told him my name and begged his forgiveness for my impertinent curiosity. He came, as I very well knew, from an upper-class family descended from warriors, and he was my senior in Karate-dō. Further, he was a noted exponent of the art of stick fighting and later founded his own school of *bōjitsu*.

There was now, of course, no question of his pulling the jinriksha while I rode in it. Walking side by side to Shuri, we had a most agreeable conversation about karate and the art of stick fighting. Then, obviously much embarrassed by my having learned his identity, he asked me not to mention to anyone that he had been working as a jinriksha man. He had, he told me, an ailing wife who was bedridden, and in order to support her and himself and buy her the medicine that she required, he worked as a farmer during the day and pulled a jinriksha by night.

Had he desired fame and fortune, he could certainly have acquired it, but possibly at the expense of engaging in work that he would have felt to be beneath his dignity. In this he was, as the saying goes, every inch a samurai, and the deft manner in which he handled the jinriksha revealed his expertise in the martial arts. Although he

Gichin Funakoshi, who was a scholar of the Chinese classics as well as a karate master, was born in Shuri, Okinawa Prefecture, in 1868 and died in Tokyo in 1957.

At Keio University's dōjō around 1930: Master Funakoshi and students practice the kata Heian Nidan.

Master Funakoshi blocks a stick attack with the weapon known in the Okinawan dialect as a *sai*. (Around 1930.)

Seen above with Gichin Funakoshi are his daughter, son-in-law and two of his grandchildren. Below, he poses with friends; the man sitting behind him is Yukio Togawa, wildlife photographer and prize-winning author.

A student's understanding of Karate-dō can be seen in his performance of the kata. Seated on the master's right are Genshin Hironishi and, next to him, Shigeru Egami, the master's successor as chief instructor of the Shōtō-kai.

As proven by medical statistics, the bending and stretching of the arms in karate forges stronger elbows than any other sport does. The photos below are of Master Funakoshi's arm.

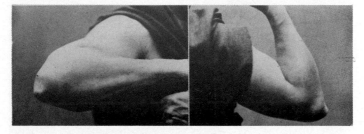

died soon after I left for Tokyo, I have never forgotten that evening spent in his company. To me he has always represented the perfect embodiment of the samurai spirit.

Spirit of the Game

The tug of war, a popular sport on our island, is usually engaged in during one of our numerous festivals. Our tug of war is quite different from that practiced in other prefectures. For one thing, it is a great deal more dynamic, as anyone who has ever witnessed an Okinawan tug of war will agree. And it is most definitely not, I assure my readers, a sport for children.

Two lengths of rope are joined to form one very long rope that is almost as thick as the trunk of a large tree. Each rope has a large loop at one end, and after one loop is slid through the other, a heavy oak bough is used to lock the two pieces together. Numerous smaller ropes dangle from the main rope, making it look rather like an enormous centipede; these smaller ropes are called *mezuna* ("female ropes"). It is the duty of the referee to insert the oak bough through the loop. Although this task is often quite dangerous, it is a ceremony that must never be omitted from an Okinawan tug of war.

The game starts when the referee stamps on the feet of the two men of the opposing teams who are nearest the center of the rope. Then all the opponents grasp the smaller "female" ropes and start tugging away to the accompaniment of drums and gongs. Cheering sections hoist banners bearing the names of their teams and urge them on by making as much noise as they can.

Although it is a game and a sport, it is also an imitation

of war and there are times (if the decision of the referee is disputed) when a real battle erupts. Many an Okinawan has been injured in the fistfights that so frequently follow a tug of war. For this reason, the referee must be a man recommended by both sides; he must also be a man capable of acting both as a referee in the sport and as a mediator in the fight that may well ensue.

In the ancient royal capital of Shuri, the tug of war has been a popular sport for centuries. Then, with the Meiji Restoration, Naha was made the capital of Okinawa and soon outgrew its older sister. During my years as a schoolteacher in Naha, I was often asked to serve as referee in tugs of war, and I am happy to report that not once did a contest that I refereed erupt into a bloody battle. What I learned from observing these tugs of war is that the team that is intent only on winning will usually fail to do so, while the team that enters the contest in order to enjoy the sport without worrying too much about winning or losing will frequently emerge victorious. The observation holds as true for a karate bout as for a tug of war.

Karate Saves My Life

Another karate story I would like to recount took place at the port of Naha, which is the most important in Okinawa Prefecture. Unfortunately it was so shallow that large ships could not pull up to the pier. They had to anchor out in the middle of the harbor, and boarding passengers were ferried out in smaller boats.

The day that I left Okinawa for Tokyo was quite windy, and the waves were high. Along with a group of other

66   TRAINING FOR LIFE

passengers, I boarded a small boat to be taken out to a large passenger ship headed for the national capital. As we arrived, the sea was momentarily calm, and several passengers stepped easily from the smaller boat onto the gangway leading up to the deck of the larger ship. When it came my turn to step from the bobbing boat, however, there was suddenly a large wave, so naturally I waited until the sea seemed calm again.

As soon as it did, I put one foot onto the gangway, but just at that very moment another huge wave came, and the ferryboat began rocking wildly. And there was I, one foot on the gangway, one still in the ferryboat, and two bulky, heavy briefcases in my hands. Beneath me was a heavy sea. To make matters worse, I must confess that, although an islander, I had never learned to swim, having been brought up in the castle town of Shuri and having seldom made excursions to the Okinawan shore.

As I stood there straddling the heaving sea, I could hear the crew of the larger ship shouting instructions down at me, but the instructions simply did not penetrate. Without thinking, I shifted the briefcase that I had been holding in my left hand over to my right and simultaneously chucked the heavier case in my right hand onto the gangway. The momentum carried me as well onto the safety of the gangway. Had I hesitated even a moment longer, I would surely have been pitched into the sea and might have drowned. And had I been rescued, it would have been with a bellyful of salt water. As I climbed the gangway, I murmured a word of thanks to Karate-dō for my close escape.

Some years later, on a return visit to Okinawa, I of course went to pay my respects to Master Azato. "Welcome back!" he cried. "But really! How frightened we were that day!" He, with his family, had come to the pier to see me off, and now they told me how terrified they had been at what might have happened. "How we admired your quickness and your skill," he added. "And how relieved we were!"

It is not, of course, karate alone that trains a man to the point where he may perform extraordinary feats of this sort; the other martial arts are equally useful. Judo experts, for example, learn to take falls in such a way that they may rise quite uninjured; this ability they all attribute to their judo training. The important point is that daily practice in any of the martial arts may turn out to be invaluable to a man in times of emergency.

RECOGNITION

Difficult Days

It was, as I recall, toward the end of the year 1921 that the Ministry of Education announced that a demonstration of ancient Japanese martial arts was to be held the following spring at the Women's Higher Normal School (then located at Ochanomizu in Tokyo). Okinawa Prefecture was invited to participate in the demonstration, and the Department of Education asked me to introduce our local art of karate to the Japanese capital. I agreed immediately, of course, and began to make plans.

Since karate was then little known outside of Okinawa, and since the people to whom it was to be presented had little or no knowledge of it, I decided that something quite dramatic was needed in the way of an introduction. What I did, accordingly, was to take photographs of the various stances, kata, movements of the hands and feet, and to arrange the photographs on three long scrolls. These I brought with me to the capital. The entire demonstration turned out to be a great success, but I think that this was particularly true of my introduction of the Okinawan art of karate to the people of Tokyo.

I had planned to return to my native island immediately after the demonstration but postponed my return when the late Jigorō Kanō, president of the Kodokan judo hall, asked me to give a brief lecture on the art of karate. I hesitated at first, not feeling myself to be sufficiently knowledgeable, but because Kanō was so earnest, I agreed to demonstrate some kata for him. The scene was to be the Kodokan itself, and I had thought that only a very small group, consisting probably of the senior teaching staff of the hall, would be present for my performance. To my considerable astonishment, there were over a hundred spectators waiting there when I arrived.

For my partner in the demonstration I had chosen Shinkin Gima, who was then studying at Tokyo Shōka Daigaku (now Hitotsubashi University). Gima was a first-rate karateka, who had practiced intensively before leaving Okinawa. Much impressed, Kanō asked me how long it would take to master the kata that we had demonstrated.

"At least a year," I replied.

"Ah, that's too long," he said. "Could you teach me only a few of the most basic ones?"

A mere provincial schoolteacher, I felt greatly honored by this request from a great judo master like Jigorō Kanō, and so of course I agreed.

Some time later I was again preparing to return to Okinawa when one morning I was called upon by the painter Hōan Kosugi. He told me that some time back when he visited Okinawa on a painting expedition, he had been deeply impressed by karate and wanted to learn the art but here in Tokyo could find neither teachers nor books of instruction. Would I, he asked, consider remaining in Tokyo some time longer and giving him personal instruction?

So once again I put off my departure and began giving lessons to members of a painters' group called the Tabata Poplar Club, of which Kosugi was president. After a number of sessions, it suddenly dawned on me that if I wanted to see Karate-dō introduced to all the people of Japan, I was the man for the job, and Tokyo was the place to start. So I wrote to Azato and Itosu telling them of my idea, and both masters replied with letters of encouragement, at the same time warning me that I would be in for a difficult time.

In this, as it turned out, they were more than right. I moved into the Meisei Juku, a dormitory for students from Okinawa (located in the Suidobata area of Tokyo), where I was permitted to use the lecture hall of the dormitory as my temporary dōjō when it was not being used by the students. However, money was a critical problem: I had none of my own, my family in Okinawa was quite unable to send me any, and I could not at that time attract any sponsors, since karate was still virtually unknown.

To pay for the tiny room where I slept, I took on all sorts of odd jobs at the dormitory: watchman, caretaker, gardener, even room sweeper. At that time I had very few students, so of course the fees I was paid were not enough to make ends meet. To help solve the problem of getting enough to eat, I persuaded the dormitory cook to take karate lessons, and in return he allowed me a discount on my monthly food bills. It was a difficult life, but when I think back about it after all these years, I realize it was also a good one.

And it was not without its lighter moments. In those days, personal interviews in newspapers and magazines were rare, but one day a newspaper reporter appeared at the dormitory. As he approached, I happened to be sweeping the garden path, and he obviously took me for a servant.

"Where can I find Mr. Funakoshi, the karate teacher?" he inquired.

"One moment, sir," I replied and scurried away. I went quickly up to my room, changed into my formal kimono, and then descended to the entranceway where the reporter was waiting. "How do you do?" I said. "I'm Funakoshi." I shall never forget the expression of astonishment on the reporter's face when he realized that the gardener and the karate teacher were one and the same!

Another time I was called upon by one of the upper servants from the house of Baron Yasuo Matsudaira, which was situated next door to our dormitory. The Matsudairas were, of course, a family of importance, and the baron and his wife were Princess Chichibu's foster parents.

"I have come," said the servant, "to thank the elderly man in the dormitory who sweeps the ground in front of our gate every morning. My master sends this small token of gratitude." With that, he handed me a box of sweets.

The epilogue to the story came a few years later when the same servant visited me again to apologize for having called me "the elderly man who sweeps the ground." He continued, "At the time, of course, we had no idea that you were the noted karate expert, Gichin Funakoshi."

It is true that the grounds of the dormitory required a great deal of attention, for children often came there to play. After a backbreaking hour of cleaning up after them, I would sometimes chide them, telling them it was all right to play in the garden but that it was by no means all right to litter the grounds.

One day one of them, a sharp-tongued little devil, called me *karasu-uri* ("snake gourd"), and then the rest of the boys took up the chorus. It all seemed rather mysterious to me, and I could not understand why I was being likened to a snake gourd until that evening, when I looked into a mirror and burst out laughing as I saw the resemblance. Although I do not drink alcohol, my complexion is quite ruddy, and as my skin is also extremely smooth, I could understand how, in that little boy's mind, I looked like a melon that becomes bright orange when ripe.

So to my students I was the karate expert, but to the Matsudaira household I was just an elderly sweeper, while to the gang of children who played in the garden I was a snake gourd. I found all this greatly diverting; what I found less diverting were the days of penury when I could not scrape up enough money to buy the necessities of life.

One day I found I would have to pawn something or other, but the question was what. I possessed hardly anything worth pawning. Finally I found an old derby I had worn in Okinawa and a hand-woven Okinawan kimono. These I wrapped up carefully and went trudging off to a distant pawn shop, for I wanted none of the students in the dormitory to know about it.

Indeed, I was ashamed even to show the two objects to the clerk in the pawnshop, for both were old and worn and, I feared, quite worthless. But the clerk carried them into a back room of the shop, where I could hear two men (the other presumably the proprietor of the shop) talking in whispers. After a few moments, the clerk reappeared and handed me an astonishingly large sum of money.

I was much mystified until I learned later that the clerk's younger brother was one of my karate students. Indeed, now that I think back upon those years, I recall a number of kind benefactors, among them Hōan Kosugi

and the other painters of the Tabata Poplar Club, and
to all of them I feel an abiding sense of gratitude.

Public Interest

As time passed, my situation began to improve. For one
thing, I was now teaching an increasingly large number
of students. Many were white-collar workers, who after
their day's work was done would come to my dōjō for a
couple of hours of practice. Eager to improve their knowledge of Karate-dō and to perfect their skills, they were
extremely enthusiastic, and it was largely thanks to them
that the art was becoming better and better known to
people in all walks of life.

Even the universities began to take an interest in karate,
with Keio in the vanguard. One day Professor Shin'yō
Kasuya, of the department of German language and lit-
erature, came to my dōjō with a couple of other members
of the Keio faculty and several students who wanted to
learn karate. Not long after that, the university formed a
karate study group made up of both faculty members and
students: this was the first group of its kind ever established
at a Tokyo university. So now, in addition to teaching at
my own dōjō, I made regular visits to the Keio campus to
give instruction in the art. Soon students from another
university, Takushoku, which was not far from the dormitory, also began coming for instruction.

On one of those increasingly busy days, a splendidly
attired gentleman appeared at my dormitory escorting a
youth in a student's uniform. I was requested to give a
brief karate demonstration, after which the youth enthu-
siastically declared his intention to study the art. It turned

out that he was Kichinosuke Saigō, a member of an aristocratic family who, after the Second World War, was elected to the House of Representatives.

As I recall, the young gentleman was at that time a student at the Peers' School. Nevertheless, he took up residence at the Tōgō-kan lodging house, which was located near my dōjō, because he was determined to spend as much time as possible in karate practice. When I told the proprietor of the Tōgō-kan that he had an aristocratic lodger, he was very much surprised and soon arranged for the young gentleman to move to another boardinghouse in Myogadani, saying that he considered it cleaner and more suitable for a nobleman's son. From this latter boardinghouse the youth, for several years, made daily trips to the Peers' School and then to my dōjō.

After the interest shown by Keio and then by Takushoku, the number of my students from various Tokyo schools seemed to grow by leaps and bounds. I recall, among others, young men from Waseda, Hosei, Nippon Medical College, the First Higher School, Tokyo Imperial University, the Tokyo University of Commerce and the Tokyo University of Agriculture. Karate study groups were, at the same time, being established at a number of institutes of higher learning. One was formed at the Nikaido College of Physical Education, and I was invited to give instruction in karate at both the military and naval academies. And I was, I may add, extremely gratified to receive visits from the parents of boys who had studied with me. They would come to thank me for the karate instruction through which their sons had become strong and healthy.

By now, of course, I had little time to sweep rooms or

gardens, nor did I have such a drastic need. In fact, one day, the proprietor of the pawn shop that had been so generous came to see me, and as he was leaving, he said quietly, "It's been so long since you've come to my shop I feared you might be ill. I am relieved to see you looking so hale and hearty!"

My wife, during all this time, was still in Okinawa, although my oldest son had come to Tokyo before I did, and my two younger sons came after my arrival. I had decided not to return to Okinawa until my mission was accomplished, and, despite the difficulties, I was confident that I could support my family in Tokyo. But this was not to be. When I wrote my wife to join me, she firmly refused.

In Okinawan religion, the veneration of ancestors is a very important element, and my wife, a devout Buddhist, would not entertain the idea of moving our ancestral grave to an unknown place. In her reply to my request, she said that it was her duty to remain in Okinawa to attend to her religious duties. I, she said, should concentrate my efforts in my work. Seeing that there was no way of changing her mind, I agreed to this, although it was to mean many years of separation.

My First Book

It was not long after I arrived in Tokyo that Hōan Kosugi, the painter, urged me to write a reference book on Karate-dō. This, I knew, would be no easy task, for, as I have noted before, there was no written material available in Tokyo and virtually none even in Okinawa. So I began by writing to masters Azato and Itosu, as well as other friends and colleagues in Okinawa, asking them to send me whatever information and ideas they could on the art of Karate-dō. But of course, when it came to writing the book, I had to rely almost entirely on my own personal experience during the days I was training and practicing the art in Okinawa.

Published by Bukyosha in 1922, the book was entitled *Ryūkyū Kempo: Karate*, and to introduce it I had the honor of including brief forewords by a number of eminent people. Among them I may mention the names of Marquis Hisamasa, the former governor of Okinawa, Admiral Rokurō Yashiro, Vice Admiral Chosei Ogasawara, Count Shimpei Goto, Lieutenant General Chiyomatsu Oka, Rear Admiral Norikazu Kanna, Professor Norihiro Toonno and Bakumonto Sueyoshi of the *Okinawa Times*.

When I reread the book today, I feel rather ashamed of the amateurish quality of the writing. However, to its composition I devoted every ounce of effort I had, and so among my various publications it remains a favorite. It was beautifully designed by Hōan Kosugi himself.

The five chapters were: "What Karate Is," "The Value of Karate," "Karate Training and Teaching," "The Organization of Karate" and "Fundamentals and Kata." In an appendix to the book, I discussed the precautions a karateka should take when practicing the art. To give the reader some idea of how I felt about karate at the time, let me reproduce here the brief introduction that I wrote for this first book of mine:

"Deep within the shadows of human culture lurk seeds of destruction, just as rain and thunder follow in the wake of fair weather. History is the story of the rise and fall of nations. Change is the order of heaven and earth; the sword and the pen are as inseparable as the two wheels of a cart. Thus, a man must encompass both fields if he is to be considered a man of accomplishment. If he is overly complacent, trusting that the fair weather will last forever, he will one day be caught off guard by terrible floods and storms. So it is essential for all of us to prepare each day for any unexpected emergency.

"To remember troubled days in days of peace and to constantly train one's body and mind form the guiding spirit and character of the Japanese people.

"Today we are enjoying peace, and our country is making great strides forward in every field. Swords and lances, now virtually useless, have been stored away in our cupboards. But now the subtle art of self-defense called karate grows increasingly popular, and people have asked me time and again whether there is not some good reference book available. Even enthusiasts have written me from remote places asking for such a book. Further, the health and strength of our young men undergoing physical examinations for military service seem to deteriorate year after year. Taking all these things into consideration, I have decided to produce a reference book on karate, by means of which the sport may be spread throughout the nation and our people may be trained in both mind and body. This first poor attempt is, of course, flawed by many defects."

This book enjoyed widespread popularity and was reissued four years later by Kobundo in revised form, with its title changed to *Renten Goshin Karate-jitsu* (Strengthening of willpower and self-defense through techniques of karate). My next book, called *Karate-dō Kyōhan*, was published in 1935 and was concerned mainly with the various types of kata. (This book, also, was designed by Hōan Kosugi.)

A number of weekly and monthly magazines also began to interest themselves in karate, and while some writers tried to present a true picture of Karate-dō, others preferred to sensationalize it. In the appendix to my first book I quoted from an article that appeared in a Tokyo newspaper, in which the author declared:

"The purpose of karate is to build a strong body. It is also an art of self-defense. A highly trained karate man is said to be capable of rising from a sitting position and shattering the ceiling of a room with one kick, of crushing a bamboo stalk with one hand, of breaking two or three thick boards with a single blow of his fist, of breaking a strong rope with one stroke, of crushing a rock with his fist and of many other superhuman feats of strength. But surely such feats are beyond human ability. 'Miraculous' is the only word by which to describe them!"

Of course, as we have seen, not all such feats are beyond human ability, and to describe them as "miraculous" is absurd. But such, I am sorry to say, is the way many people regarded karate in those early days.

Friends and Acquaintances

One of the first officers of our armed forces to recognize the value of karate was Admiral Rokurō Yashiro, who had won considerable fame in the war with Russia. As the reader may recall, it was he who called at Okinawa and was so impressed by demonstrations of karate that he ordered officers and men in his command to practice it.

I have no idea how Admiral Yashiro learned that I was in Tokyo, but he did, and one day he invited me to his house in Koishikawa Hara-machi. He remembered all the things he had seen in Okinawa and told me that he himself, as well as his sons and his grandsons, wanted to learn karate, so I agreed to visit his house once a week to teach them the art.

Whenever the day of practice came, he would personally greet me at the gate of his house, wearing formal kimono, and after we had finished our practice sessions, he would see me off. We had frequent conversations both before and after the sessions, and I profited greatly from his wide experience. I found him a man much to be admired. Another naval man from whom I learned many valuable things was Isamu Takeshita, who was also later in life to attain the rank of admiral.

This may sound strange, but a number of sumō wrestlers were also acquaintances and students of mine. Uichirō Onishiki, for instance, was a famous grand champion of the time, although perhaps the younger generation of today may not remember his name. Sometimes he would bring other wrestlers of the same stable to my Meisei Juku dōjō for practice sessions, but as my dōjō was quite small and sumō wrestlers are not, I preferred to demonstrate kata at Onishiki's stable in Ryogoku. Another sumō wrestler to whom I gave frequent instruction was a champion named Fukuyanagi, who suffered an untimely death as a result of eating improperly prepared globefish. The wrestlers were always extremely attentive during the sessions, and just as they do today, they used to go on frequent tours throughout the country. But as soon as they returned to the capital they would come to my dōjō to report.

One day, I recall, Grand Champion Onishiki and I were strolling near Ishikiri bridge in Koishikawa when it started to rain. I, as it happened, had no umbrella with me, but Onishiki immediately opened his over our heads. But since Onishiki was over six feet tall, while I was a mere five-footer, his umbrella was not doing me much good. Seeing this, he insisted upon my taking the umbrella with the words, "If you please." He himself draped a hand towel over his head as we continued walking.

After his retirement, Onishiki opened a restaurant in Tsukiji, where he invited me to dine one evening. He offered me a cushion to sit on while he himself sat directly on the straw mat, thus adhering strictly to the etiquette appropriate between teacher and pupil. I could not but be deeply impressed by the former grand champion's strong sense of propriety.

In addition to Onishiki and Fukuyanagi, there were half a dozen other famous wrestlers who studied karate with me, and I found that I learned much from them even as I was teaching them. My conclusion was that the ultimate aim of both karate and sumō was the same: the training of both body and mind.

Shōtō-kan

It would have been difficult for any man to foresee the extent of the catastrophe that struck Tokyo on the first day of September, 1923. That was the day of the Great Kanto Earthquake. Nearly all buildings were made of wood, and in the hours of raging fire that followed the quake, the great capital was reduced to ruins. My dōjō, fortunately, escaped destruction, but many of my students simply vanished in the holocaust of falling and blazing buildings.

We who survived did all we could to succor the injured and the homeless in the days immediately following the terrible disaster. With those of my students who had not been maimed or killed, I joined other volunteers to help provide food for the refugees, to clear the rubble, and to assist in the task of disposing of the dead bodies.

Of course, the task of teaching karate had to be temporarily postponed, but earning a living could not very well be deferred. After a short time, some thirty of us found work at the Daiichi Sogo Bank making stencils. I no longer remember how much we were paid or how long we kept the jobs, but, as I recall, that daily traveling from the dōjō at Suidobata to the bank at Kyobashi seemed to go on for an endless period of time.

I do remember one aspect of the daily commuting. In those days, very few people wore shoes in the streets of Japanese cities; everyone wore either sandals or the wooden clogs called *geta*. There is one type of the latter, called *hōba no geta*, that has two extremely long teeth and sometimes only one, and it was these that I always wore to strengthen my leg muscles.

I had done so as a youth in Okinawa, and I saw no reason to change now as I commuted to my job at the bank. The one-tooth *geta* I wore were carved of very heavy wood and made a loud clack at every step, as loud as that made by the metal *geta* worn by some karate trainees today. I have no doubt that passers-by in the streets looked at me with hidden laughter, amused that a man of my years should be so vain as to want to add to his height. After all, I was well over fifty years old at that time. I

82   RECOGNITION

assure my readers, however, that my motive was not vanity: I considered my one-tooth *geta* a necessity for daily training.

With the passing of the weeks and months, Tokyo began to rebuild itself, and eventually there came a time when we realized that our dōjō was in a state of serious disrepair. The Meisei Juku had been built around 1912 or 1913, and nothing had been done to it for a long time. Fortunately, we were granted some money by the Okinawa prefectural government and the Okinawa Scholarship Society to make the much needed repairs.

But of course we had to find other quarters while the Meisei Juku was being refurbished. Hearing that I was now in need of training quarters, Hiromichi Nakayama, a great fencing instructor and a good friend, offered me the use of his dōjō when it was not being used for fencing practice. Initially I rented a small house near Nakayama's dōjō, but soon I was able to rent a larger one with a large yard where my students and I could practice.

The time came, however, when this arrangement was inadequate. The number of my students increased, but so did the number of fencing students. The effect of this was that I was inconveniencing my benefactor. Unfortunately, my financial situation was still poor and I could not do what was obviously desirable: construct a dōjō specifically for karate.

It was around 1935 that a nationwide committee of karate supporters solicited enough funds for the first karate dōjō ever erected in Japan. It was not without a trace of pride that, in the spring of 1936, I entered for the first time the new dōjō (in Zoshigaya, Toshima Ward) and saw over the door a signboard bearing the dōjō's new name: Shōtō-kan. This was the name that the committee had decided upon; I had had no idea that they would chose the pen name I used in my youth to sign the Chinese poems I wrote.

I was sad, too, for I had wanted above all for masters Azato and Itosu to come and teach at the new dōjō. Alas, neither was any longer on this earth, so on the day that the new dōjō was formally opened, I burned some incense in my room and prayed to their souls. In my mind's eye, those two great teachers seemed to smile at me, saying, "Good work, Funakoshi, good work! But don't make the mistake of complacency, for you still have much to do. Today, Funakoshi, is only the beginning!"

The beginning? I was then nearly seventy years old. Where would I find the time and the strength to do all that still needed to be done? Fortunately I neither looked nor felt my years, and I determined, as my teachers demanded of me, not to give up. There still, they had told me, was much to do. Somehow or other, I would do it.

One of my first tasks, with the completion of the new dōjō, was to make up a set of rules to be followed as well as a teaching schedule. I also formalized the requirements for the grades and classes (*dan* and *kyū*). The number of my students began to increase day by day, so that our new dōjō, which had seemed more than adequate for our needs at the start, now grew progressively less so.

Although, as I say, I did not feel my years, I realized that I could not possibly fulfill all the duties that were steadily accumulating. Not only was there the dōjō to be managed but also Tokyo's universities were now forming karate groups in their departments of physical education, and these groups needed instructors. Clearly, it was too much for one man to oversee the dōjō and travel from university to university, so I appointed advanced students to teach at their own universities in my place. At the same time, I took on my third son as my assistant, delegating to him the daily tasks of running the dōjō, while I supervised the teaching both there and at the universities.

I should point out that our activities were not confined to Tokyo. Many graduates of my dōjō as well as karateka from the universities took jobs in provincial cities and towns, with the result that karate became known all over the country and a large number of dōjō were built. This gave me yet another mission, for as karate spread I was constantly being besieged by local groups to travel here and there to give lectures and demonstrations. When I was to be away for any length of time, I left the running of the dōjō in the good hands of my senior students.

I am often asked how I happened to choose the pen name of Shōtō, which became the name of the new dōjō. The word *shōtō* in Japanese means literally "pine waves" and so has no great arcane significance, but I should like to tell why I selected it.

My native castle town of Shuri is surrounded by hills with forests of Ryukyu pines and subtropical vegetation, among them Mount Torao, which belonged to Baron Chosuke Ie (who, as a matter of fact, became one of my first patrons in Tokyo). The word *torao* means "tiger tail" and was particularly appropriate because the mountain was very narrow and so heavily wooded that it actually resembled a tiger's tail when seen from afar. When I had time, I used to walk along Mount Torao, sometimes at night when the moon was full or when the sky was so clear that one stood under a canopy of stars. At such times, if there also happened to be a bit of wind, one could hear the rustle of the pines and feel the deep, impenetrable mystery that lies at the root of all life. To me the murmur was a kind of celestial music.

Poets all over the world have sung their songs about the brooding mystery that lies within woods and forests, and I was attracted to the bewitching solitude of which they are a symbol. Perhaps my love of nature was intensified because I was an only son and a frail child, but I think it would be an exaggeration for me to term myself a "loner." Nevertheless, after a fierce practice session of karate, I liked nothing better than to go off and stroll in solitude.

Then, when I was in my twenties and working as a schoolteacher in Naha, I would frequently go to a long, narrow island in the bay that boasted a splendid natural park called Okunoyama, with glorious pine trees and a large lotus pond. The only building on the island was a Zen temple. Here too I used to come frequently to walk alone among the trees.

By that time I had been practicing karate for some years, and as I became more familiar with the art I became more conscious of its spiritual nature. To enjoy my solitude while listening to the wind whistling through the pines was, it seemed to me, an excellent way to achieve the peace of mind that karate demands. And since this had been part of my way of life from earliest childhood, I decided that there was no better name than Shōtō with which to sign the poems that I wrote. As the years passed, this name became, I think, better known than the one my parents gave me at birth, and I often found that if I did not write Shōtō along with Funakoshi people were apt not to know who I was.

ONE LIFE

Great Losses

On the far horizons of Manchuria and Mongolia the clouds of war were gathering, but the sky over Japan itself was still blue and peaceful. Life went on as it always had, with the emperor carrying out his many official functions. I was most closely touched by his annual presence at karate demonstrations, for I was once granted the honor of being one of the demonstrators.

I still vividly recall every single moment of that day when I, with half a dozen of my students, performed karate kata in the imperial presence. The impoverished Okinawan youth who used to walk miles every night to his teacher's house could hardly have foreseen, even in his dreams, such a highpoint in his karate career. Yet here it was, and the honor, for me, was heightened by the fact that I could indeed perform the kata before His Majesty although I was now well past fifty years of age.

I had, to be sure, performed in the imperial presence before, when the emperor was crown prince and had called at Okinawa on his voyage to Europe. But the situation then was very different. At that time, karate was one of the least known of the martial arts; in fact, I think it is safe to say that it was hardly known at all outside the Ryukyuan Islands. But now it had taken its place along with the other traditional martial arts, and as I considered the tremendous difference between that distant Okinawan day and this day in Tokyo, I found it very hard to contain my emotion.

After the demonstration I was invited to a gathering by Suteki Chinda, then grand chamberlain to the emperor. He told me that His Majesty recalled well that demonstration at Shuri Castle and had asked whether the leader on that occasion was not the same man who had just performed at the Imperial Palace in Tokyo. The reader may well imagine my feelings on hearing this.

Our peaceful days were now drawing to a close. As the Manchurian Incident began to broaden in scope, Japan embarked upon preparations for a full-scale war. Now the number of students coming to my dōjō grew even greater; and after the actual outbreak of hostilities with China, which was soon to be followed by the great Pacific War, my dōjō could no longer contain the number of young men who desired to train. As they practiced in the yard and even out in the street, I feared that the sound of their bare fists pounding straw-padded posts would be a nuisance to the neighbors.

"*Sensei*," I would often hear a young man say as he knelt before me, "I have been drafted, and I'm off to serve my country and my emperor." Every day I would hear my students, often more than one, report to me in this fashion. They had been strenuously practicing karate day after day in preparation for hand-to-hand encounters with an unmet enemy, and they believed that they were ready. Indeed, I was told that some officers instructed their men, if they were unable to carry a rifle or a sword, to charge the enemy with their bare hands. This came to be known as a "karate charge."

Of course many of my students died in battle—so many,

alas, I lost count of them. I felt my heart would break as I received report after report telling me of the deaths of so many promising young men. Then I would stand alone in the silent dōjō and offer a prayer to the soul of the deceased, recalling the days when he had practiced his karate so diligently.

And of course, like so many others my family and I suffered our personal misfortunes, misfortunes that intensified as it became increasingly evident that the Pacific War would end in Japan's defeat. When, in the spring of 1945, my third son, Gigō, was taken ill and had to be hospitalized, I moved in with my oldest son in Koishikawa. While I was living there my dōjō was utterly demolished in an air raid.

I thought about how it had been built with love and generosity by friends of Karate-dō. It was a crystallization of their devotion to the art, and it seemed to me the most wonderful thing that I had ever accomplished in my life. Now, between one moment and the next, it was gone.

Soon, of course, there was a far greater catastrophe to be endured: the emperor issued his decree accepting defeat. The chaos of life in Tokyo that followed surrender was more than I could bear, so I left for Oita, in Kyushu, where my wife had fled when the fierce battle for Okinawa began. At least, I thought, I could live quietly with her, and at least I would have a better chance of getting enough to eat there than in the hunger-haunted metropolis.

But life in Kyushu was not quite what I had anticipated. For one thing, there had been a mass evacuation from Okinawa to Oita, and neither my wife nor I had any relatives among the hordes of refugees. Nor was there very much to eat: a few vegetables that we grew ourselves and seaweed that we gathered for ourselves at the shore. My wife, old as she was, retained her indomitable spirit—but not, to my intense sorrow, for very long.

One day she fell suddenly ill. She had always suffered from asthma, and now it grew so bad she could hardly breathe. As I sat with her one afternoon, I saw her lift her wasted body in the bed and turn her face in the direction of Tokyo. I watched her lips move in silent prayer. Then she turned again, this time toward Okinawa, clasped her trembling hands, and breathed another silent prayer. I knew, of course, what was in her mind: when she looked toward Tokyo she thought of the emperor and the Imperial Palace; she thought of her children and her grandchildren; and when she looked toward Okinawa she offered her last prayer to the ancestral spirits before joining them herself.

So my wife died, she who through the long years had done everything possible to help me and encourage me in my devotion to karate. Ever since I moved to Tokyo, around my fiftieth year, I had been separated from her, and when, in the years before, we had been together in Okinawa, her life had been far from easy. We were so very poor that neither she nor I could enjoy many of the ordinary pleasures of life that are the solace of the average couple. She gave her whole life to me, her husband, with his love for karate, and to her children.

I believe her extraordinary qualities were recognized by the people of Oita, for they made a most unusual exception for her in their long-established funeral tradition. It is a strange fact that the village funeral homes are only for the bodies of people actually born in Oita. Bodies of strangers are relegated to a town-operated mortuary in

Usuki. But village dignitaries succeeded in arranging for my wife to be cremated at a local funeral home, and it was, I think, the first time in the history of the village that such an exception was made. It was a touching tribute to her memory, to her special human qualities.

The time was late autumn, 1947. In a few days I left for Tokyo clutching an urn that contained the ashes of my wife. I was going to stay for a time at the home of my oldest son. As the ancient wartime train crawled slowly toward Tokyo, it stopped at numerous stations. To my great surprise, at each station there were former students of mine who had come to greet me and offer condolences. I do not know how they knew I was on the train nor how they knew about the death of my wife, but I was terribly touched by their solicitude. Tears flowed down my cheeks unchecked until there came the realization that she had died as nobly as she had lived.

Recognizing True Karate

More and more, in recent years, I have heard people say, "karate sannen-goroshi" or "karate gonen-goroshi," meaning that a man who has been struck by a karate blow will inevitably die either three years or five years after the blow. This sounds quite savage and is of course wholly deplorable, but inasmuch as there is some truth in it, I should like to go into the matter here very briefly.

To be sure, it is altogether inaccurate to say that if you strike an opponent in a certain way, he is inevitably doomed to death within a period of three or five years. But it *is* true that a man so struck, although he may not die at the moment he is hit, may after some years actually die as a result of the blow. Certain karate blows, then, may tend to shorten the life of the victim: therein lies the modicum of truth that has given rise to these pronouncements.

How does this come about? No doubt all my readers have seen photographs of karateka breaking boards or tiles with a blow of their bare hands. Generally the first board or tile remains undamaged while those beneath are the ones that get broken; the broad that actually receives the blow shows no sign of having been struck.

The same may be true of a blow to the human body: nothing appears on the surface of the body, but the interior may be seriously damaged. We have all heard of instances in which a man has been struck by something but, feeling little or no pain, dismisses the matter. Then, as time passes —perhaps years—the pain begins, and may increase. But striking such blows, like breaking boards and tiles, is far from the true essence of Karate-dō.

Let us say that a person skilled in karate can usually break about five boards with a single blow. Now if the average man who knows absolutely nothing of karate undergoes sufficient training he will probably be able to break three or four boards. But we certainly may not say that he has therefore come to understand the true meaning of karate. Should he attempt to utilize the ability he has thus acquired by initiating attacks on others, he would in all probability lose the fight; he has succeeded in strengthening his hands but he has failed to understand the nature of karate.

I recall how fearful the Metropolitan Police Department was (at the time I first came to Tokyo) that karate might be used as an offensive weapon. People are not, I think, so foolish today. Some years later, a high-ranking officer said to me, "You know, anyone found carrying a gun or a sword may be arrested for illegal possession of weapons, but with karate the only weapons are hands and legs, and we can hardly arrest people for carrying those. So I should like to ask you to caution the young men training at your dōjō not to make use of their skill for any illegal purpose. There are so many gangs of hoodlums in the country today!"

I realized that if through my efforts such gangs learned karate and made use of it to maim or even murder people, my name would be disgraced forever. I am proud of the fact that out of the tens of thousands who have studied and practiced the art of karate at my dōjō, I know of not one single instance in which the skill has been used illegally.

I have always stressed the point in my teaching that karate is a defensive art and must never serve offensive purposes. "Be careful," I wrote in one of my early books, "about the words you speak, for if you are boastful you will make a great many enemies. Never forget the old saying that a strong wind may destroy a sturdy tree but the willow bows, and the wind passes through. The great virtues of karate are prudence and humility."

That is why I teach my students always to be alert but never to go on the offensive with their karate skills, and I instruct my new students that I will under no circumstances permit them to use their fists to settle personal differences. Some of the younger ones, I confess, disagree with me: they tell me that they believe karate may fairly be used whenever circumstances make it absolutely necessary.

I try to point out that this is a total misconception of

the true meaning of karate, for once karate enters, the issue becomes a matter of life and death. And how can we allow ourselves to engage in such life and death confrontations often in our few years on earth?

Whatever the circumstances, karate must not be used offensively. To illustrate my point, I give the example of a young man who had spent but a short while at my Meisei Juku dōjō and who one day decided to try his kick on the dog that patrolled the grounds of the Matsudaira residence next door to us. The young man's kick failed, and he was himself seriously bitten by the dog. So I say that those who, having trained in karate, think they must put their skills to use pervert the meaning of the art.

Another phrase I should like to comment on here is the so-called karate chop used in professional wrestling. It is not, actually, a subject I am very well qualified to speak of, for I know little or nothing about professional wrestling, and since I dislike being part of a crowd, I have never seen a match except on television.

This "karate chop" is the chief weapon employed by Rikido-zan, the man most directly responsible for the popularity of professional wrestling in Japan today, for which I respect him. I wondered where he had learned karate and was told that when he was a sumō wrestler he studied with Yukio Togawa, who had earlier trained at my dōjō. Thus, Rikido-zan studied karate before taking up professional wrestling, a fact that clearly illustrates how determined he was to learn all the skills of his trade.

When I saw his famous "karate chop" on television, I realized that it is nothing but a variation of the *shutō* blow in karate. The word *shutō* means "sword hand," referring to the use of the hand as a sword or knife, with the four fingers and the thumb extended and held close together.

Despite their apparent similarity, however, the "karate chop" and the shutō are two very different things. When I watched Rikido-zan on television, he seemed to be wielding his hands rather in the manner that children swing a bamboo "sword." Our shutō, however, is a far more lethal weapon: it is like a sharp steel sword. A shutō blow to the side of an opponent's neck has the ability to kill him instantaneously. If it strikes the shoulder blade, it will shatter the bone; and it can, like the blade of a knife, pierce the body of an opponent. It is this same shutō that is sometimes used to break boards and tiles.

Despite the fact that the "karate chop" is a descendant of the shutō blow, the experienced karate man will see a number of differences. In karate, for instance, the arm is seldom raised high above the head (although beginners are told to do so in practicing the kata so as to make their movements freer). But an adept will never raise his arms high, as the wrestler does with his "karate chop."

Further, the latter is made with the arm almost fully extended, while the shutō blow is delivered with the elbow bent. Since it is made without opening the sides wide, the physical movement involved is rather small when compared with that of the "karate chop," but it can of course be infinitely more lethal.

Every Day

I am often asked by reporters (and even, in fact, by members of the medical profession) that question that we older people must get used to answering. To what, everyone wants to know, do I owe my longevity? And my candid answer is that I have no secret prescription—except moderation. Although I am ninety years old, I feel in such good health and spirits that I would not be at all surprised if today marked the beginning of a new life for me!

Moderation, yes. Nevertheless, I think that perhaps if I tell my readers about some of my lifelong daily habits, they will understand more clearly how it has been possible for me to live to such a ripe and active old age. As I recounted at the very beginning of this book, my birth was premature, and so my own family as well as their acquaintances in the neighborhood anticipated that I would not survive more than three years. Now, ninety years later, I still teach karate and write books and my mind is as busy thinking up new activities as though I were only half my present age.

Let us look for a moment at the important subject of food. I eat sparingly, never to the point of being full. Vegetables are a favorite item in my diet, and although I am fond of meat and fish I eat both with restraint. I make it a rule never to have more than one side dish and never more than one bowl of soup. I think restraint in the matter of food may be one of the chief reasons I have kept my excellent health. I may also mention that it is my custom, and always has been, to eat hot meals in summer and cold ones in winter. For example, I never, as most people do, eat ice cream or sherbet in hot weather.

As for dress, I dislike heavy clothing. Okinawa, of course, is very warm most of the year around, so there is little need for heavy clothes, but even today, in our Tokyo winters, I dress as lightly as possible. I have never made use of those charcoal braziers we call *hibachi* or the charcoal

ONE LIFE

heaters (*kotatsu*), nor have I ever bothered with anything like a hot-water bottle.

During all the four seasons of the year, I sleep on a single, thin mat, with a wood or rattan pillow, and even in the depths of winter I cover myself with only a single quilt. I have never used extra blankets. Because my family was poor, I early grew accustomed to this relative austerity, and have never seen any good reason to change my way of life. Even today I live in a rented house, and what is more I insist upon an upstairs room. This I do very deliberately, because I believe that climbing stairs is excellent training for the leg muscles. This habit, too, may be an important factor in my lifelong good health.

I always rise early. I suppose my young readers, who are used to having things done for them, may find this astonishing, but the moment I rise I roll up my quilt and tuck it away in the cupboard. When I lived in Okinawa, I never allowed my wife to perform this chore for me, nor would I now let my children or grandchildren do it. My custom has always been to do things for myself, such as sweeping my room, or airing my quilt, or dusting my books. I am a firm believer in the importance of cleanliness, and I insist upon performing the chores that make for cleanliness myself. Such has always been my custom.

Upon rising, I brush off any dust that may have settled upon the portrait of Emperor Meiji in court dress, a portrait that was given me by my children, or upon that of Takamori Saigō, the Meiji statesman and soldier. The latter was presented to me by his grandson, Kichinosuke Saigō. This done, I sweep my room, practice some kata, wash my hands and face, and then eat my simple breakfast.

I now occasionally allow myself an indulgence that I would not have considered when I was younger: I sometimes take a brief nap before my noon meal. My afternoons are often given over to calligraphy or reading. The calligraphy is usually the result of requests from students who, having graduated from university, have entered upon occupations in outlying districts and wish me to write some kind of motto for them.

I have practiced calligraphy since childhood, but never then did I permit anyone else to prepare my ink for me, nor do I do so now. As my readers may know, Japanese calligraphers use sticks of solid pigment that they turn into ink by rubbing them against a stone bowl containing water. This is a slow process, so I am often several months late in fulfilling requests from former students. I do hope they realize that it is not my years that cause the delay!

I find when doing calligraphy I have no need for eyeglasses but do need them when it comes to reading letters written in pen and ink. My auditory sense is still keen enough, but I must confess that my teeth are not my own. I have no trouble with them when I eat, but I have found that sometimes during a conversation they grow loose and I fear they may fall out, so I press them against my gums with a finger, which does not always contribute to intelligibility. I believe I shall have to buy myself a new and better set one of these days.

Well, after all, a man can hardly reach my age without other people noticing. Sometimes I twit my eldest son's wife with the words: "Caution your husband to be careful when he goes to the city—there are so many cars and buses on the streets, and your man's not getting any younger!"

"And how old," she rejoins tartly, "do you think *you* are, grandfather?"

Two habits I have never acquired are smoking and drinking. When I was a young lad, my karate teachers warned me against both, and I have faithfully followed their admonition. "If you happen to be with ten companions," said one teacher, "or twenty, or fifty, never forget that they may all, if they get drunk, turn into enemies. Should you drink, always bear this in mind."

One lifelong habit that I have maintained is taking a daily bath, but unlike most of my fellow countrymen I prefer moderately warm water to very hot. Nor do I like to linger long in the water. In the past, when I used to go to the public bath, the attendant would offer to give me a massage, but I found it always made me feel ticklish, so I would soon ask him to stop. Now the young folk in my family ask me if I would like a massage, but I refuse, telling them that, old as I am, my muscles are in excellent condition.

And that is true, although perhaps strangers, seeing me walking down the street, would not think so, for I still use the sort of gliding walk that we call *suriashi*, which was the style when I was young. Young people unacquainted with this old-fashioned custom might suppose me weak in the knees, but they would be wrong.

I travel alone, making frequent trips to Kamakura, for example. I need no assistance boarding or alighting from trains, and I truly find it regrettable that the universities always send a car for me when I go to lecture to the students. Regrettable too is the fact that when on one of my solitary jaunts I happen to encounter a former trainee, he will invariably insist upon accompanying me to my destination. It is, of course, a great kindness, but, although my hair is white and in but a single decade I will be a centenarian, I feel no need of anyone's assistance.

My chief regret is that my memory is simply not so keen as it once was. I sometimes forget things or make silly mistakes, like getting off at the wrong train station, but younger people, I think, sometimes commit similar errors, so I refuse to accept this as proof of senility.

This failure of memory extends also to the students in the karate departments of the various universities. There are so many of them! And sometimes I forget not only their names but even which universities they are attending. While they are still students, wearing student uniforms, the matter is relatively simple, but it is less so after they graduate and start wearing ordinary clothes.

Sometimes men whom I taught decades ago visit me when they come to Tokyo. Of course they recall me quite vividly, but the numbers of my former students run into the tens of thousands. So frequently I do not know what to call them, and am forced to fall back on that standard phrase, "How tall you have grown!"

Then the youngsters in my family nudge me and murmur, "Grandfather, your guest is a handsome and prosperous gentleman. Don't you think it's rather impolite to tell him that he's grown up?" But whether I remember them clearly or not, I am always happy to receive visits from my former students, and I am most grateful to them for helping to popularize Karate-dō.

One of my chief pleasures now is being in the company of young karate enthusiasts. A few years ago, four or five, I was invited to Shimoda, in Izu, by such a group. I took the train to Itō and then the bus, and when my young

ONE LIFE

hosts met me I think they expected to find me dead tired.

With tender care they conducted me to the hotel where a room had been reserved for me on the ground floor. I asked the manager instead for an upstairs room because of the view and because, as I told him, I would feel better when I woke. He was happy to oblige, but this became another source of apprehension to my young hosts as well as to the hotel staff, all of whom were fearful that I might stumble and fall on my way downstairs. So I had to demonstrate to them that a man of ninety can still climb stairs and descend them too.

The inhabitants of the town, I learned, thought I must be at least twenty years younger than I actually was, and the entire trip to Shimoda was a pleasant one indeed. My hosts seemed to have enjoyed it as much as I did. The memory of their smiling faces, which was with me all the way back, made me realize my life's work was far from finished. Although Karate-dō has seen great progress, it is not yet so popular as I would like. Thus I feel I must go on living quite a while longer to see the completion of the work that I set out, long ago, to do.

Courtesy

Some youthful enthusiasts of karate believe that it can be learned only from instructors in a dōjō, but such men are mere technicians, not true karateka. There is a Buddhist saying that "anyplace can be a dōjō," and that is a saying that anyone who wants to follow the way of karate must never forget. Karate-dō is not only the acquisition of certain defensive skills but also the mastering of the art of being a good and honest member of society.

We greet our friends by saying "good morning" or "good afternoon," and we remark upon the weather. This is quite ordinary, and we hardly think about it, but should we not think about something that is rather more important?

In our present time of liberalism and democracy, I shall no doubt be accused of conservatism, even of being a reactionary, if I suggest that the courtesy we show our neighbors and acquaintances should also be extended to the members of our families. This is what I do believe, however—that we should show more concern for our parents and grandparents, for our brothers and sisters. It is a matter so obvious that we often forget.

The young in particular ought to show greater concern for their families, and this, obviously, is a matter of importance not only to would-be practitioners of karate but also to every member of the human race. The mind of the true karateka should be imbued with such concern before he turns his attention to his body and the refinement of his technique. Love of karate, love of self, love of family and friends: all lead eventually to love of one's country. The true meaning of karate can be acquired only through such love.

Let us, as an example, take one of the commonest everyday occurrences, the visit to the public bathhouse. I daresay no one has escaped the unpleasant experience of finding the dipper or wooden basin he is about to use half-full of dirty water, which means that before using it himself he has to clean up someone else's dirt. The person who preceded him was clearly one who lacked ordinary politeness. Some people bring their hand towels into the communal tub and actually go so far as to wash themselves in water that other people are soaking in. Some men who wish to shave find that the mirror is being used and so, instead of waiting until it is free, engage in the dangerous practice of shaving without getting a clear view of what they are doing. Anyone with ordinary politeness will, after he has dressed, take the three or four steps necessary to put the basket that had contained his clothes back in its orginal place, rather than leave this to be done by the bath attendant. The public bath is one of the best places in the world for a man to demonstrate, in the course of his daily life, what he truly is.

I no longer remember how long ago it was that I happened to read the autobiography of the late Seiji Noma, founder of Kodansha (the publishing house), but I have never forgotten the book, and I realize that I learned a great deal from it.

One passage in particular struck me. "I used to go to the public bathhouse every evening," he wrote. "Whenever I entered, the attendant would greet me with the word 'Welcome,' and whenever I left he would say, 'Thank you very much.' For a long time I did not bother to reply to his greetings, but suddenly I realized that it would be courteous to do so."

He went on to underline the importance of always replying to such greetings, and I decided to put his advice into practice that very day. Entering my bathhouse, I heard a word of welcome, at which I smiled and said, "Good evening." The attendant, more than a little surprised at my unaccustomed reply, returned my smile. When I left, I said "Goodnight" in answer to his "Thank you very much." After that, the attendant and I became quite friendly. The tone of his voice, which previously had been little more than perfunctory, grew warmer and more personal, and the visit to the public bath became, for me, more than just daily routine.

One of the things I always tell my new students is that he who thinks about himself alone and is inconsiderate of others is not qualified to learn Karate-dō. Serious students of the art, I have discovered, are always highly considerate of one another. They also demonstrate the great steadfastness of purpose that is essential if one is to continue studying karate over the long period of time that is required.

Each year, in the month of April, a great number of new students enroll in the karate classes of the universities' physical education departments—most of them, fortunately, with the dual purpose of building up their spiritual as well as their physical strength. Nonetheless, there are always some whose only desire is to learn karate so as to make use of it in a fight. These almost inevitably drop out of the course before half a year has passed, for it is quite impossible for any young person whose objective is so foolish to continue very long at karate. Only those with a higher ideal will find karate interesting enough to persevere in the rigors it entails. Those who do will find that the harder they train the more fascinating the art becomes.

IMPORTANT POINTS

Six Rules

To be sure, the best way to understand Karate-dō is not only to practice the kata but also to gain an appreciation of the meaning inherent in each of the various kata. However, since I have treated the kata at some length in *Karate-dō Kyōhan* and they are not the subject of this book, here I should like only to mention six rules, the strict observance of which is absolutely essential for any man desirous of understanding the nature of the art. [Although Master Funakoshi speaks of "six" rules, the one numbered three is unaccountably missing.]

1. You must be deadly serious in training. When I say that, I do not mean that you should be reasonably diligent or moderately in earnest. I mean that your opponent must always be present in your mind, whether you sit or stand or walk or raise your arms. Should you in combat strike a karate blow, you must have no doubt whatsoever that that one blow decides everything. If you have made an error, you will be the one who falls. You must always be prepared for such an eventuality.

You may train for a long, long time, but if you merely move your hands and feet and jump up and down like a puppet, learning karate is not very different from learning to dance. You will never have reached the heart of the matter; you will have failed to grasp the quintessence of Karate-dō. To be deadly serious, then, is not just an es-

105

sential for a follower of Karate-dō; it is equally essential in everyone's daily life, for life is itself a struggle to survive. Anyone so complacent as to assume that after a failure he will have another opportunity will seldom make much of a success of his life.

2. Train with both heart and soul without worrying about theory. Very often a man who lacks that essential quality of deadly seriousness will take refuge in theory. Let us say, as an example, that a man has been practicing a particular kata for a couple of months and then he says with a weary sigh, "No matter how hard I train, I cannot master this kata. What shall I do?" A couple of months! How could he master a kata in a couple of months?

The *kibadachi* ("horse-riding stance"), for instance, looks extremely easy but the fact is that no one could possibly master it even if he practiced every day for an entire year until his feet became as heavy as lead. What nonsense, then, for a man to complain after a couple of months' practice that he is incapable of mastering a kata!

True practice is done not with words but with the entire body. Others have mastered the kata that you are practicing. Why then are you unable to? Is there something wrong with you? These are the questions you must ask yourself; then you must train until you fall from exhaustion; then soon you must continue, using the same strict regimen. What you have been taught by listening to others' words you will forget very quickly; what you have learned with your whole body you will remember for the rest of your life.

Karate-dō consists of a great number of kata and basic skills and techniques that no human being is capable of assimilating in a short space of time. Further, unless you understand the meaning of each technique and kata, you will never be able to remember, no matter how much you practice, all the various skills and techniques. All are interrelated, and if you fail to understand each completely, you will fail in the long run.

But once you have completely mastered one technique, you will realize its close relation to other techniques. You will, in other words, come to understand that all of the more than twenty kata may be distilled into only a few basic ones. If therefore you become a master of one kata, you will soon gain an understanding of all the others merely by watching them being performed or by being taught them in an instruction period.

I shall tell an old story here that I think well illustrates my point. It concerns a very famous reciter of ballad-dramas, who had a very strict teacher when he was learning the art in his youth. Day after day, week after week, month after month, in fact year after the year, the young man was made to recite the very same passage from the *Taikōki* ("the story of Toyotomi Hideyoshi") without ever being permitted to go any further.

Finally despair overwhelmed the young man, who (if I recall correctly) was destined to become the famous Master Koshiji. Persuading himself that he was not suited to the profession, he ran off one night from his master's house, heading for the shogun's capital of Edo and some other profession.

Following the Tokaido road, Koshiji stopped one night at an inn in Shizuoka Prefecture where, as luck would have it, a recitation contest was to be held that very evening. Having nothing to lose, Koshiji entered the contest and recited, of course, the passage from the *Taikōki* that he knew so well. After he had finished, the sponsor of the competition cried out his admiration. "That was superb!" he exclaimed. "Do tell me who you are, for I am sure you are a very famous master."

Young Koshiji was pleased by these words of praise, but at the same time, somewhat perplexed, he had to confess that he was a mere beginner. His astonished listener replied, "I find that very difficult to believe. You performed this evening like a famous master. Under whom, then, do you study?"

At this, Koshiji spilled out the story of how he had run away because his master was so very demanding.

"Ah, what a terrible mistake you have made!" cried the sponsor. "It is precisely because of that demanding teacher of yours that you have been able to recite so superbly this evening after studying for only a few years. If you will take my advice, go back at once to your teacher, offer him your apologies, and beg him to resume your instruction."

Young Koshiji did so, and before he died became the most famous master of his time. I tell this little story not merely, of course, to inspire reciters of ballad-dramas, nor even would-be followers of Karate-dō; I tell it because, like the lesson of so many stories that may or may not have their basis in actual events, it is applicable to life itself.

4. Avoid self-conceit and dogmatism. A man who brags in booming tones or swaggers down the street as though he owned it will never earn true respect even though he may actually be very capable in karate or some other martial art. It is even more absurd to hear the self-aggrandizing of one who is without capability. In karate it is usually the beginner who cannot resist the temptation

to brag or show off; by doing so, he dishonors not only himself but also his chosen art.

5. Try to see yourself as you truly are and try to adopt what is meritorious in the work of others. As a karateka, you will of course often watch others practice. When you do and you see strong points in the performance of others, try to incorporate them into your own technique. At the same time, if the trainee you are watching seems to be doing less than his best, ask yourself whether you too may not be failing to practice with diligence. Each of us has good qualities and bad; the wise man seeks to emulate the good he perceives in others and avoid the bad.

6. Abide by the rules of ethics in your daily life, whether in public or private. This is a principle that demands the strictest observance. With the martial arts, most particularly with Karate-dō, many neophytes will inevitably exhibit great progress, and in the end some may turn out to be better karateka than their instructors. All too frequently I hear teachers speak of trainees as *oshiego* ("pupil"), or *montei* ("follower"), or *deshi* ("disciple"), or *kohai* ("junior"). I feel such terms should be avoided, for the time may well come when the trainee will surpass his instructor. The instructor, meanwhile, in using such expressions runs the risk of complacency, the danger of forgetting that some day the young man he has spoken of rather slightingly will not only catch up with him but go beyond him—in the art of karate or in other fields of human endeavor. The familiar tale of the tortoise and the hare applies not only to children. I often tell my young colleagues that no one can attain perfection in Karate-dō until he finally comes to realize that it is, above all else, a faith, a way of life.

When a man enters upon an undertaking, he prays fervently that he will achieve success in it. Further, he knows that he needs the help of others; success is not to be attained alone. With Karate-dō, by extending help to others and by accepting it from them, a man acquires the ability to elevate the art into a faith wherein he perfects both body and soul and so comes finally to recognize the true meaning of Karate-dō.

I should like to think I am mistaken, but I am afraid I am not, for all too often recently I have heard young karate trainees use such expressions as *jitsuryoku-gata* ("a man of real ability"), or *sentō-gata* ("a man of battle"), or *jissen-gata* ("a man of actual combat"). These terms are absurdly childish and betray an abysmal ignorance of the meaning of Karate-dō.

Inasmuch as Karate-dō aims at perfection of mind as well as body, expressions that extol only physical prowess should never be used in connection with it. As one Buddhist saint, Nichiren, has so aptly said, everyone who studies the Sutras should read them not only with the eyes that are in his head but also with those of his soul. This is the perfect admonition for a trainee of Karate-dō to always keep in mind.

Violating a Rule

I must now confess that I have been known to lapse from strict observance of the rules. This particular incident occurred a few years after the end of the Pacific War.

Being only about eighty years old at the time, I was rather more active than I am now, and so one day I went to a poetry-reading party in Tamagawa. As there was a good deal of drinking (to help celebrate an anniversary), the party lasted quite late, and I was just in time to catch the last train back to Tokyo.

Japan, then, was still in a state of postwar chaos, and people were warned that it was dangerous to walk alone at night. But I decided no one would molest an old man like me, so after getting off the train at Otsuka Station I started for home. This part of Tokyo was ruined and deserted, while the house where I was living, which luckily had escaped any actual bombing, was still some distance away.

It now started to rain, so I pulled up the collar of my coat, opened my umbrella, and began to walk. The incident I am about to relate occurred somewhere between Otsuka and Hikawashita; it began when a black-clad figure sprang suddenly out from behind a telephone pole. "Hey, Granddad!" he cried, making a lunge for my umbrella.

Thinking he must be a friend or an acquaintance, I backed away courteously and removed my hat so as to bow to him.

This seemed to astonish him. Then, after a moment's silence, he said in rather an uncertain voice, "How about a cigarette, Granddad?"

I now realized that he was a thief but I could also tell, from the tone of his voice, that he was a very amateur one—a newcomer to the trade, so to speak, trying to pretend that he was tough.

"I don't smoke," I replied.

I should explain that I never carry a briefcase. That night, wrapped in my plain dark *furoshiki*, all I had was my now empty lunchbox and some books.

"What's the idea of lying, Granddad?" asked the man. "You've got some cigarettes in your *furoshiki*."

"I have already told you that I don't smoke. Now will you kindly let me pass?"

"Never mind about that!" the man cried. "Untie your *furoshiki* and let's see what's in it!"

"There's nothing in it of the slightest value," I said.

"That's what you say!" With that, the man snatched my umbrella from my hand, and it looked to me as though he was about to try to hit me with it.

His stance was full of openings. When he swung the umbrella at me, I ducked under and, with my right hand, took a firm grasp of his testicles. The pain was, I have no doubt, very nearly unbearable. The umbrella fell to the ground, and the man himself, after a sudden sharp cry, looked as though he might well pass out.

Just at that moment, fortunately, a patrolling police officer appeared on the scene, and I released my assailant into his custody.

As I continued on my way, I realized that the would-be robber was almost certainly a veteran recently returned from some distant front. Jobless, he had decided to rob me on the spur of the moment, and I, also on the spur of the moment, had done what I constantly tell my young trainees never to do: I had taken the offensive.

I did not feel very proud of myself.

Karate for Everyone

One of the most striking features of karate is that it may be engaged in by anybody, young or old, strong or weak, male or female. Further, one need not even have an opponent for practice purposes. Of course, as one progresses in the art, an adversary will be essential in order to practice sparring (*kumite*) and free sparring (*jiyū kumite*), but a real adversary is unnecessary in the beginning. Nor is there any need for a specially made uniform. Even a dōjō is unnecessary: a person can practice karate in his own yard. Of course, anyone truly determined to master the various kata must do so at a proper dōjō, but someone whose desire is merely to stay healthy and to train his mind and spirit may do so by practicing karate by himself.

For all these various reasons, then, we find that there are many more women practicing the art now than formerly, which I think is an advantage both for the women themselves and for Karate-dō. But if college girls who study karate refrain from publicizing the fact, I think we who have been responsible for its propagation may also be responsible for fostering the idea that it is an art to be practiced only by men.

Yet even if the general public tends to think poorly of women who choose to study karate, the women themselves find the art just as intriguing as men do. One reason, I think, is that the kata are graceful movements, not unlike those used in various kinds of dancing. On television now we see what are called "beauty exercises" for women, and I have thought, watching them, how effectively our karate kata could be utilized for this purpose, since they can be practiced anywhere.

Frequently I have been asked whether a woman who has learned karate will not want to dominate her husband after marriage. The contrary is far more likely to be the case, I would say; a karate-trained wife will make all efforts to obey her husband because karate begins and ends with courtesy. A wife who has followed Karate-dō would not dream of trying to prevail over her husband.

We know very well that karate can improve the appearance of girls and young women, so much so that parents have frequently brought their children to me to be taught the art. On numerous occasions, I have accepted sickly young girls as pupils, only to see them recover their health after six months or so of training—but by then karate has come to mean so much to them that they have no desire to give it up.

There is also the indisputable fact that a woman with some knowledge of karate can defend herself against even a powerful male assailant. However, on this point I would like to reiterate that karate is not, and never has been, merely a brutal form of self-defense. On the contrary, anyone who has truly mastered the art of karate will take care not to venture into dangerous places or situations where he or she may be forced to put the art to use. Just as a karate-trained man will not go looking for a fight, so a karate-trained woman will not put herself into a position where she must use her skill to subdue a would-be rapist.

One thing I often say to my young pupils they find confusing. "You must," I tell them, "become not strong but weak." Then they want to know what I mean, for one of the reasons they have chosen Karate-dō is to become strong. It is hardly necessary, they tell me, to train in order to become weak. Then I reply that what I am saying is indeed difficult to understand. "I want you to find the answer within yourselves," I tell them. "And I promise you that the time will come when you truly understand what I mean."

114   IMPORTANT POINTS

I am convinced that it will. I am convinced that if young people practice karate with all their heart and all their soul, they will eventually arrive at an understanding of my words. He who is aware of his own weaknesses will remain master of himself in any situation; only a true weakling is capable of true courage. Naturally, a real karate adept must refine his technique through training, but he must never forget that only through training will he be able to recognize his own weaknesses.

THE PAST, THE FUTURE

Many Weapons

Many people are under the erroneous impression that karate weapons consist only of the hands (clenched or unclenched) and the arms, the feet and the legs. It is no exaggeration, however, to say that every part of the body, from the top of the head to the tips of the toes, may be used as a weapon. For example, from the wrist down there are at least ten potential weapons: the *seiken* (regular fist), the *uraken* (the back fist), the *shuken* (the hand-fist), the *ippon-ken* (the single-point fist), the *chūkōken* (another single-point fist), the *tettsui* (the hammer-fist), the *shutō* (the sword hand), the *nukite* (the spear hand), the *ippon nukite* (the one-finger spear hand) and the *nihon nukite* (the two-finger spear hand). And from the ankle down: the *koshi* (the ball of the foot), the *shusoku* (the hand-foot), the *sokutō* (the sword foot), the *tsumasaki* (the tip of the toe), the *enju* (the heel) and the *sokkō* (the top of the foot). Other areas of the arms and legs used as weapons are the wrists, the elbows and the knees. There is almost no part of the body that may not be used as a weapon.

I should like now to describe very briefly which parts are used most frequently and also how effective they can be. For those who practice karate merely as a form of calisthenics, I should also like to give a brief explanation of how those various parts may be strengthened through training.

116

We must begin, certainly, with the *seiken*, the regular fist, for this is the most basic of all karate weapons, the one most frequently employed. It is formed by clenching the four fingers against the palm and then inserting the thumb between the index and middle fingers. Should you insert the thumb any more deeply, you may injure it when you use the seiken in striking a blow; therefore, care must be taken to ensure that it never goes any further than the middle finger.

The knuckles form an acute rather than a right angle. In the beginning you will find it difficult to form such a fist and you will tire after a moment or two, but with continued practice you will become used to it and grip your fist more tightly. Further, the knuckles will become highly developed and will form into a thick lump rather like a callus, while the bases of the fingers will, at the very least, make right angles. With highly trained experts, the angle becomes acute.

One very good time to practice the making of a seiken is while you are in the bath. Coat your hands with soap, so as to make your fingers slippery; then practice clenching and unclenching your fists, in the manner described, as often as possible.

The novice will find when he tries to deliver a thrust punch with the seiken that his hand bends at the wrist. A thrust punch made with a bent fist is never a highly effective blow. Further, there is always the danger that the beginner delivering such a blow may sprain his wrist.

When the seiken is used correctly, the knuckle of the middle finger strikes the opponent in one straight blow, with all the force of the arm behind it. The seiken may properly be called the heart of karate and should be practiced every day and with the utmost thoroughness. Unless it is completely effective, all kata and *kumite* become worthless.

The most popular way of training with the seiken is to make use of a *makiwara*, a thick post covered with rice straw. The *makiwara* also, incidentally, may be used in strengthening the sword hand (shutō), the elbows and the knees. I think I am in no way exaggerating when I say that practice with the *makiwara* is the keystone in the creation of strong weapons.

About seven feet tall and about six inches in width, the wooden makiwara is stuck firmly in the ground until the top of it reaches roughly to the height of the practitioner's shoulders. Then rice straw is wound around the upper part of the stave to a thickness of about two or two and a half inches; the straw is secured by thin ropes. At first the beginner, in striking the straw-padded stave, will experience considerable pain in his fists, so I recommend that initially a towel be wrapped over the straw.

Once the makiwara has been prepared, the trainee takes a half-facing position (*hanmi*) in front of it, ensuring that the distance between him and the stave is short enough so that his fist may reach the target. He bends his knees fully and drops his hips low. His left hand is clenched and thrust forward to a distance of about six inches from the makiwara, while his right hand, also clenched, is at his hip, the palm facing downward. His eyes are fixed upon the makiwara, and his power is concentrated in the lower abdomen (the *tanden*). The straw-padded part of the makiwara should be on a level with his chest, for if it is higher he will have to spring upward and so lose power.

The most important point is the stance: the legs must feel as though they are firmly rooted to the ground. Now comes the blow itself. The clenched right fist, which has been held close to the side of the body, is thrust out; simultaneously, the right hip is turned toward the target with all one's power while the clenched left fist, which had been poised some six inches from the makiwara, is drawn back to the left side. When making the actual strike, the right fist should be rotated quickly in a corkscrew motion just as it touches the target. In other words, it is a corkscrew punch, and that makes the blow all the more lethal. This is a very difficult action to master, so the trainee must practice it over and over again.

I would suggest that the beginner strike the makiwara weakly at first, increasing the power gradually until his fist has grown accustomed to absorbing a strong blow. Eventually, of course, the trainee will be able to strike with all his might. Even if the beginner strikes the makiwara only very lightly, he may still experience pain and soreness in his hand, or he may merely graze his target (although it stands but three feet away), as a result of which his hand may become bruised or swollen. The swelling will be alleviated by soaking the hand in ice water, but broken skin will necessitate postponing training until the wound is healed.

To repeat two or three points of great importance about the seiken: the stance must be a low one, the hips must turn quickly and powerfully, and the fist must eventually bring to bear all the strength of which the body is capable. One further observation: any trainee who is heard to boast that calluses have formed on his knuckles has not yet learned the meaning of Karate-dō. Incidentally, anyone who practices karate as a form of calisthenics need not use a makiwara: he may practice and go through all the necessary actions without ever striking a blow.

In addition to the seiken, another important punch is that administered by the back fist (*uraken*), in which that part of the fist that strikes the opponent consists primarily of the knuckles of the first and second fingers. However, if a man is training with a makiwara, he must take care that the knuckles of all four fingers hit the target. The *uraken* is a highly effective weapon for hitting the face, for striking below the armpits, and for punching the sides of the torso should an opponent attack from the side.

Then there is the hammer-fist (*tettsui*). The thumb is clenched between the two fingers as in a seiken, but the part of the fist that strikes is not the same. Here it is the padded cushion of the palm that lies just beneath the little finger. Many claim that this is not a very effective blow, but I can assure my readers that a tettsui fully developed with the use of a makiwara is a very strong weapon indeed. Inasmuch as the part of the area that actually strikes the target is very soft, it will not be injured to any great extent no matter how hard the target is. For that reason, the tettsui may be most effectively used for striking an opponent's wrist or other joints.

The spear hand is a weapon that penetrates the opponent by making use of the tips of the fingers. The *shihon nukite* utilizes all four fingers, the *nihon nukite*, two, and the *ippon nukite*, one. The thumb is bent inside the palm while the fingers are extended and held close together. Someone unacquainted with this blow might suppose that the fingers could be seriously damaged when striking the opponent, but the fact is that with sufficient practice the nukite is a highly useful weapon against both the face and the solar plexus.

The shutō, or sword hand, which I have already described briefly, has numerous applications. It is formed in the same way as the *shihon nukite*, except that the striking area is the soft cushion of the palm under the little finger. The makiwara is very helpful in strengthening this weapon. The shutō may be used most effectively against the opponent's neck, side, arms and legs.

Empi means the elbows, which are used frequently, both offensively and defensively—when your opponent tries to grab hold of you, for example, or when he attacks from either side or front, or when you crouch low to get inside his defense, or when you grasp your opponent to bring him in close to you. The elbows are effective in striking an opponent's face or head, chest, sides or back. They may also be used to protect your own chest and sides, and if you are thrown to the ground, your elbows are useful in striking at your opponent's legs. Because the elbow bones are strong, women and children also may, with sufficient practice, make highly efficient use of the elbows.

Leg and foot motions, provided they are fast enough, are among karate's most important weapons, for they frequently take the opponent by surprise. Leg action consists mainly of kicking, but sometimes the legs and feet are used for blocking. The legs are, of course, thicker and stronger than the arms but are more difficult to use effectively without considerable practice. There is a serious danger too: if a man kicks out with one leg and misses his target, he will be off balance, providing his opponent with an opening for kicking him in return.

The word *koshi* refers to a particular area of the sole of the foot that is used to strike a frontal opponent. The formation is similar to that of the seiken, but it should be noted that if the foot is not pointed upward sufficiently or if sufficient power is not concentrated in the ankle, then the *koshi* becomes a source of danger to its user. The heel (*enju*) is useful against an opponent who attacks from the rear or attempts to grasp the body from behind.

Recollection of Childhood

Before bringing to a close these all too random reflections about Karate-dō and myself, I should like to say a few words about another local Okinawan sport, not only because it provided me with many hours of fun when I was young but also because I believe it helped me develop that muscular strength that is so useful in karate.

The sport I am talking about is wrestling. But, you will say, people wrestle all over the world. Children begin to play at wrestling almost as soon as they are old enough to play at anything. Ah, but Okinawan wrestling has certain unique features. As with karate, its origins are unknown, and many Okinawans suppose that there must have been a relationship of sorts between the two.

The Okinawan name for our style of wrestling is *tegumi*, and should you write the word, you would use the same two Chinese characters that are used to write karate's *kumite*, except that they are reversed. Tegumi is, of course, a far simpler and more primitive sport than karate. In fact, there are few rules except for certain prohibitions: the use of fists, for example, to strike an opponent, or the use of the feet and the legs to kick him. Nor are opponents

122

permitted to grab each other's hair or pinch one another. Prohibited also are the sword hand and the elbow blow used in karate.

Unlike most forms of wrestling, in which the participants are lightly clad, entrants in tegumi bouts remain fully clothed. Further, there is no special ring; the bout may be held anywhere—inside the house or in some nearby field. I should note that when I was young the outdoors was generally the scene for tegumi bouts because they tend to get rather lively and our parents did not like to see sliding paper doors and tatami mats damaged. Of course, when we held a bout in a field, we first had to remove all the rocks and stones that are a prevailing feature of the Okinawan rural scene.

The bout begins, as sumō does, with the two opponents pushing against each other. Then, as it proceeds, grappling and throwing techniques are used. One that I recall well was very similar to the *ebigatama* (leg block and three-quarter Nelson) of today's professional wrestling. When I watch wrestling on television nowadays, I am often reminded of the tegumi of my Okinawan youth.

The referees were usually boys who acted also as seconds to the opponents, their principal role being to ensure that neither participant was seriously injured or knocked unconscious. To stop the fight, all that any boy who felt he had had enough needed to do was to pat his opponent's body. Some boys, however, were so dauntless that they would go on fighting until they were knocked out. In such cases, it would be the duty of the referee to try to stop the bout before that happened.

Like every other Okinawan boy, I spent many happy hours engaging in or watching tegumi bouts, but it was after I had taken up karate seriously that I came to realize that tegumi offers a unique opportunity for training, in that it need not be limited to two participants. One (usually, of course, an older and stronger boy) may take on two or three opponents or as many as he feels up to.

Such bouts begin with the lone wrestler lying down flat on his back, his opponents pinning down his arms and legs. Once I had determined to become a karateka, I used to get four or five younger boys to wrestle with me, believing that such bouts would strengthen my arm and leg muscles as well as those of the stomach and the hips. I cannot now say how much tegumi actually contributed to my mastery of karate, but I am certain that it helped fortify my will.

For example, I seldom had any great difficulty thrusting back a single opponent, but my difficulties increased greatly as the number of my opponents increased. Then, if I attacked one opponent, the others would find an opening in which to attack me. It is hard to think of a better way than this to learn how to defend oneself against more than one opponent, and if it sounds like nothing but a children's game, I can assure you that those of us who engaged in it took it very seriously.

From what I hear, tegumi is once again becoming popular with the children of Okinawa—and the thought does not make me happy at all. The reason is that where we used to casually chuck rocks and stones out of the way to make an arena for ourselves, the children in today's Okinawa may instead encounter shells or unexploded bombs left over on that bloody battlefield of the Pacific War. That possibility is a very heartbreaking thing to ponder.

Karate Becomes International

Before the war, very few non-Japanese knew anything about, or had a desire to learn, karate. Those who did find their way to my dōjō were either reporters or physical education instructors who had heard about the Japanese interest in karate. With the end of the war came the occupation, and then a number of American soldiers began to visit me and to ask for instruction in karate. How they came to hear about me I do not know.

One day I was taken by the late Bunshiro Suzuki to the Imperial Hotel to meet an American publisher. At that time, Japanese were not permitted to enter the Imperial except at the invitation of some American who was staying there. So I was more than a little surprised, when I entered the room where we were to meet, to find it decorated in the Japanese manner, with folding screens and flowers that had clearly been arranged by some student of ikebana. My chief memory of that meeting is the American gentleman's astonishment at my rather advanced age. His remark on the subject, as it was translated for me, was to the effect that while we in Japan were turning Karate-dō from a martial art into a sport, in America it would be valued as a key to longevity.

After that I had a number of other experiences with visiting and occupying Americans, and I soon became accustomed to seeing foreign faces (including even a few female ones) at the dōjō of the Karate Kyōkai. I was asked to teach karate to the physical education officer at the U.S. Air Force base in Tachikawa, and a little later I was asked to demonstrate kata for the commander of the base in Kisarazu, Chiba Prefecture.

On the latter occasion, the commander, although he obviously knew little or nothing about karate, asked me to perform it in truly Japanese fashion. He welcomed me most cordially, watched the demonstration with great respect, and himself saw me off the base. Before doing so, he took me to a shrine on the base dedicated to Japanese airmen killed in combat.

There was a monumental bronze statue of a youthful Japanese airman pointing out toward the Pacific Ocean, an eagle with outspread wings at his feet. Both the shrine itself and the *torii* that led to it were in immaculate condition. The commander told me that he had not had it removed out of respect for the young Japanese fliers who had given their lives for their country, although those lives had been given in vain. He then asked whether any former students of mine had been wartime pilots. When I bowed deeply toward the shrine, he understood my reply, and he himself saluted. Here, I thought, was a true gentleman, and it was with tears in my eyes that I bade him farewell at the gateway to the base.

After the treaty of peace between Japan and the United States was signed, karate made its own peaceful way to the American mainland. This was brought about when I was asked by a high-ranking American officer to make a three-month tour of mainland bases, demonstrating Karate-dō to American airmen. To assist me I chose Isao Obata (of Keio University), Toshio Kamata (of Waseda) and Masatoshi Nakayama (of Takushoku). To make the tour we had a special plane put at our disposal, and instead of demonstrating before small groups of spectators, as before, we were now practicing our kata before large numbers of interested American airmen. I cannot express the pleasure I felt.

So Karate-dō which, in my childhood, was a clandestine local Okinawan activity, had finally become one of Japan's martial arts before it took wings and flew to America. Now it is known all over the world. As I write these notes, I receive requests for information, and for instructors too, from everywhere. Still astonished by the number of people who have heard about karate, I now realize that once this book is finished I shall have to start a new project—that of sending Japanese karate experts abroad.